PROFESSIONAL ETHICS

PROFESSIONAL ETHICS

POWER AND PARADOX

Karen Lebacqz

———

ABINGDON PRESS
NASHVILLE

PROFESSIONAL ETHICS

Copyright © 1985 by Abingdon Press

Library of Congress Cataloging in Publication Data

LEBACQZ, KAREN, 1945–
  Professional ethics.
  Includes index.
  1. Clergy—Professional ethics. 2. Professional
  ethics. I. Title.
  BV4011.5.L43   1985   253   84-11148

ISBN 0-687-34325-9

MANUFACTURED BY THE PARTHENON PRESS AT
NASHVILLE, TENNESSEE, UNITED STATES OF AMERICA

For Dale,
For Sharon,
and
For all the students from
CE 120: Professional Ethics

CONTENTS

INTRODUCTION: THE CROQUET GAME

RUTH is an associate minister serving her first appoint-ment in a suburban church. Like many "associate" ministers, her primary responsibility is the youth group.[1]

A fifteen-year-old high school junior from the group appears at Ruth's office door one day. Obviously upset, the young woman blurts out, "I need to talk to somebody, but you mustn't share this with *anyone*."

Sensing her deep distress, Ruth replies, "Kathy, what happens here in this office is just between us. Please tell me what's troubling you."

Kathy bursts into tears. "I'm pregnant, and I've got to have an abortion. My parents would kill me if they knew. My boyfriend doesn't know and I don't ever want to see him again. I've missed two periods and I don't have enough money to pay for the abortion. Please help me."

This is a true story. It happened a few years ago. It is not unusual. It typifies the ethical dilemmas that ministers face every day.[2] Novice or seasoned veteran, every parish minister confronts similar ethical dilemmas. And such dilemmas push to the very roots of what it means to be in the profession.

What should Ruth do? Should she help Kathy secure an abortion? Should she lend her money if needed? Should she keep confidence?

Does it make a difference that Kathy is only fifteen? that she is a member of the youth group? that her parents might be opposed to abortion? that Ruth explicitly says the information will not go beyond the walls of the office? Does it make a difference that Kathy divulges this information to Ruth in her office, because of her work with the youth group—in short, in her professional role? Does it make a difference that Ruth is a woman breaking into a profession dominated by men? that her job might be on the line depending on what she decides? that she is an "associate" minister with collegial obligations toward her senior colleague? Does it make a difference that Ruth's job description includes not only youth work but calling and preaching—hence, direct responsibilities toward the adults of the church as well as the youth?

This book is written for "Ruth" and for all professionals seeking a framework for making ethical decisions. It is for "helping" professionals who experience doubt, anxiety, or curiosity about their roles and seek guidance for the ethical dilemmas they face every day. It is also for laypeople and clients who are concerned about whether the care they receive is unethical or unprofessional. But above all it is for clergy[3] and for clergy-in-training whose need for guidance in professional ethics has been sadly neglected.[4]

What should Ruth do? How should she decide which course of action to take? What factors count in the decision? Taking a specific focus on the issue of confidentiality, I hope to suggest some factors that should weigh in Ruth's decision. It is not my intention here to resolve all aspects of Ruth's dilemma, but only to suggest a framework for ethical decision making.

Throughout this study, I will ask: Does it make a difference to confront this dilemma as a professional? I hope to show that it does. Utilizing a "praxis" approach—reflecting on an actual dilemma and utilizing theory in the light of that dilemma—I find that traditional approaches to professional ethics are not sufficient. The role of the professional and the place of professionals in society make a difference and must be taken into account. The structures of professional practice make a difference and must be taken into account. The character of the professional and her story make a difference and must be taken into account. An adequate framework includes reflection on action, character, and structure. All must figure somehow.

But just how is not easy to determine. The field of ethics itself is being shaken and tumbled about today. Though many agree that we need a systematic approach to roles and the obligations that derive from them,[5] very little attention has been given to this question. Traditional approaches that focus on rules and their application are being challenged by approaches that deal with stories, character, and structures.[6] Thus, to suggest a framework for making ethical decisions is already to plunge into an enormous debate within the field of ethics.

In addition, taking seriously the role of the professional is no simple matter. The professions are under attack today.[7] Can the concept even be used meaningfully? In spite of a growing interest in professional ethics, there is no agreement on what constitutes a profession or on the usefulness and importance of professional roles.

Indeed, some argue that ministry is not a profession. Others say it is, but disagree about its purpose and place in society.[8] The task of assessing aspects of *this* profession that might influence a framework for professional ethics is complicated.

The net result is a bit like the croquet game described in *Alice in Wonderland:*

> The chief difficulty Alice found at first was in managing her flamingo: she succeeded in getting its body tucked away, comfortably enough, under her arm, with its legs hanging down, but generally, just as she had got its neck nicely straightened out, and was going to give the hedgehog a blow with its head, it *would* twist itself round and look up in her face, with such a puzzled expression that she could not help bursting out laughing; and, when she had got its head down, and was going to begin again, it was very provoking to find that the hedgehog had unrolled itself, and was in the act of crawling away: besides all this, there was generally a ridge or furrow in the way wherever she wanted to send the hedgehog to, and, as the doubled-up soldiers were always getting up and walking off to other parts of the ground, Alice soon came to the conclusion that it was a very difficult game indeed.[9]

11

Just when one gets the field of ethics straightened out and is about to give the professions a blow with its head, the field "twists itself round," and one has to begin again. The professions, like hedgehogs, keep unrolling themselves and crawling away. Ministry walks off to other parts of the ground. There are ridges and furrows everywhere. It is, as Alice claims, a "very difficult game indeed."

In a game in which "they don't seem to have any rules in particular; at least, if there are, nobody attends to them,"[10] it is impossible to finish the game. What I propose to do is no more than to lay the groundwork for new rules and new ways to play. Taking the dilemma above as a case study, I offer a three-part framework focusing on action, character, and structures. The framework is offered in the conviction that, critics notwithstanding, there are practicing professionals who care about professional ethics and clients seeking professional services who also have reason to care. The croquet game is difficult, but I believe it is not impossible. So, let us play. . . .

PART I
ACTION

1. RULES
AND SITUATIONS

F<small>ACED</small> with an ethical dilemma such as Ruth's, we ask, What should I do? We seek appropriate *action*. The first part of a framework for analyzing ethical dilemmas must therefore clarify how to choose the right action.

One place to begin is with rules. Are there any rules to guide us or tell us what to do? Bernard Mayo suggests that the typical approach to ethical dilemmas is a two-step process: we locate a rule ("do this"; "avoid that"), and then we assume or judge that it applies to our situation. Thus, "if I am in doubt whether to tell the truth . . . to a dying man, my doubt may be resolved by showing that the case comes under a rule about the avoidance of unnecessary suffering, which I am assumed to accept."[1]

In Ruth's case, the application of a rule is very clear. Every code of ministerial ethics includes a provision binding the minister to keep confidence—for example, "The confidential statements made to a minister by his parishioners are privileged and should never be divulged without the consent of those making them."[2] A clear rule governs the professional's behavior and requires her to keep confidence. Ruth was approached in her professional work setting (her office). Kathy is a member of the youth group—a parishioner. It seems clear, then, that Ruth's code of professional ethics applies to the situation. She can point to a rule binding her to keep confidence.

Rules and Reasons

Why do we have rules, and how binding are they? Rules governing professional behavior have their own distinctive

15

histories. Some develop for particular reasons and can be traced to a time when the rule seemed necessary to define or protect professional behavior. Others develop in a more general fashion and get codified only after long years of being accepted and understood as "working rules" for conduct.

In this case, the rule that binds the minister to confidentiality has a specific history. Since the Fourth Lateran Council in 1215, the Catholic Church has required that matters communicated in confession (the sacrament of penance) were to be "under the seal."[3] Strictly speaking, this means that the lips of the priest are sealed forever. No priest can be compelled to divulge anything told to him in the confessional, and any priest who does divulge such a confidence has broken a sacred duty of the priesthood.

In Reformation tradition, confession or penance is not a sacrament. Counseling occurs under more informal circumstances rather than in the formal setting of the confessional. Nonetheless, the practical and theological underpinnings of secrecy remain.[4] Ruth is bound by church tradition and theology to respect confidences and not to divulge them.

Indeed, this strong expectation within theological tradition has given rise to some legal protections for priests and ministers. Under the "priest-penitent privilege," many states exempt ministers and priests from divulging confidential information.[5] While their provisions are often restrictive,[6] they serve the function of reinforcing the expectation that ministers will keep confidence.

There are good reasons to have and to maintain this rule. The guarantee of confidentiality encourages penitents to seek the advice, counsel, and mediated pardon that ministers and priests offer. If forgiveness of sins is integral to salvation and if clearing one's conscience is an important step in receiving forgiveness for sins, then this practice is intimately related to the salvific purposes of the church.[7] The rule that binds ministers to confidentiality facilitates a central task of ministry by encouraging parishioners to divulge their troubles and cleanse their spirits. In keeping the rule, the minister ensures that the reputation of ministry in general, and of her own ministry in particular, is maintained so that others who are troubled or anxious will also be encouraged to seek solace or professional counsel. The rule serves a teleological purpose: it encourages good relations between clients and professionals.

Kathy probably chose Ruth to confide in partly because she likes her and trusts her as a person, but partly also because Ruth is a minister—and therefore is expected to keep confidence. The minister is a "safe environment" for the adolescent to share her fears and troubles. This safety exists because of the rule that binds ministers to confidentiality. Ruth might well consider herself bound by the "seal" or duty to keep confidence, for she was acting in her role as minister and received a "penitential" communication from one of her parishioners.

The first reason for following the rule, therefore, would be recognition of the importance of the rule in establishing the practice of ministry and facilitating its goals.[8]

The second reason is avoiding harm. Once such a rule exists and the expectation of confidentiality is ingrained, to break confidence could have disastrous consequences. Adrienne Rich writes eloquently of the violation that we feel when trust is broken:

> When we discover that someone we trusted can be trusted no longer, it forces us back onto some bleak, jutting ledge in a dark pierced by sheets of fire, swept by sheets of rain, in a world before kinship or naming or tenderness exist; we are brought close to formlessness.[9]

Kathy has trusted Ruth. She indicates that Ruth is the only person she can trust in this situation. To share the information with someone else might destroy Kathy's ability to trust any adult—or any professional. Following the rule not only facilitates good relations between professional and client, but also prevents harm to the client.

Another reason for keeping confidence is to protect third parties. When Kathy divulges her own secret, she also divulges information about her boyfriend. Sissela Bok argues that "confidentiality on the part of the confessor or therapist is

17

indispensable as a protection for third .parties whose secrets are thus revealed."[10]

Adhering to the rule is also the safest course of action for the minister in some ways. Having rules to govern professional behavior keeps us from reinventing the wheel every time we make a decision. It is difficult to know ahead of time all of the possible consequences of our actions. Rules develop because the human community has found that they facilitate good consequences. Following such a rule will *tend* to facilitate good consequences, whereas the consequences of breaking the rule are less certain. We would not necessarily choose more wisely or do the right thing more often by trying to assess the consequences in each case than we would by simply honoring the rule. We might simply waste time and exhaust ourselves.[11] Rules protect us from the possible errors we would make in exercising our own judgments.

Situation Ethics

And yet, we do not think that promises should always be kept, or confidences never broken. No matter how important the rule and how strong the reasons for it, we do find justifiable exceptions. It might be wrong to break a promise for trivial reasons, but not in Kathy's very urgent situation. Though the reasons for keeping confidence in professional situations seem binding on the whole, there may be equally strong reasons here for Ruth to contemplate breaking that rule.

First, Kathy is an adolescent. It is not clear that she knows what is best for her.[12] In the panic of the moment, she may not be considering all the important factors. If Ruth has a professional obligation to seek Kathy's good, she might want to ensure a decision made with broader perspective.

Second, there is a question of potential harm to Kathy. Significant harm might be sufficient to outweigh the binding nature of the rule of confidentiality.[13] Suppose Ruth suspects that Kathy's parents would go through a time of anger and grief and would then offer support and assistance to Kathy.

Kathy may be cutting off support and help. Perhaps following the rule would be the right thing to do in most cases, but not in the rare case where the minister is quite sure that the adolescent is harming herself. If the pregnancy is getting into the second trimester, there is also the possibility of physical harm from an abortion.

Third, Kathy is still dependent on her parents and has filial obligations to them. Perhaps they have a right to know—either because of their responsibility for Kathy in general, or simply because they are "family" and their destinies are tied together in some way. What happens to Kathy will affect her entire family on some level. Perhaps, then, they have a right to be involved. As Michael Bayles suggests, "Many of the most . . . difficult problems of professional ethics concern conflicts between a professional's obligations to a client and to others."[14]

Fourth, there is Kathy's boyfriend. The child-to-be is his as well as hers. Though Kathy declares that she hates the sight of him, this does not account for his possible feelings and rights. Nor does it account for his responsibilities. If he is a member of the youth group, then Ruth has a professional relationship to him as well as to Kathy. What should she do about this relationship and about his rights and responsibilities?

Fifth, there is Ruth's colleague. Does the senior minister on the staff have a right to know simply because he is her colleague?[15] Does he need the information to facilitate his ministry to Kathy's parents? If he is not only Ruth's colleague but also her supervisor, he may be ultimately responsible for anything she does. Does he have a right to protect himself professionally—or to supervise Ruth in making a difficult decision that may affect her entire career?

Sixth, there is the church community. Church members might also claim a right to know on grounds that they are "the body of Christ" and that what affects one of them affects them all.[16] They may genuinely want to "share each other's burdens." While legal responses to abortion currently stress privacy, it is not clear that these grounds should receive theological affirmation. What is Ruth's responsibility to the church as a whole?

Finally, there is the fetus—the child-to-be. Kathy is contemplating ending its life. Some would argue that it has a right to life.[17] Should confidence be broken in order to protect this right?

In short, there are other considerations besides the expectation that ministers keep confidence. What if it seems that Ruth could do more good by breaking the rule than by following it?

This is precisely the challenge presented by Joseph Fletcher and other proponents of the "situation ethics" approach to moral decision making.[18] Fletcher argues that there are no moral rules that are absolutely binding save one: to maximize good consequences. Lying, stealing, adultery, and other activities previously prohibited by rules might now be considered acceptable. It depends on the situation—that is, on the consequences. If lying does more good than harm, it is acceptable; if adultery brings pleasure to an unbearable marriage, it is no longer to be considered wrong. Fletcher inveighs against the idea that any actions are right or wrong *intrinsically;* everything depends on extrinsic circumstances.

In Ruth's case, then, the code of professional ethics would be interpreted as a general guideline, not an absolutely binding rule. A judgment must be made in each situation about the consequences of keeping or breaking confidence. The "rightness" or "wrongness" of breaking a promise depends on the consequences, not on following a rule. If breaking the promise of confidentiality would do more good than harm for Kathy and for other parties involved, the situational approach would say, "Break the promise."

Ruth's dilemma presents a striking example of the conflict between the rule that binds us in a situation and those aspects of the situation that make us wonder whether adhering to rules is sufficient. Should the rule hold in this case? Or are the other troubling aspects of the case sufficient to outweigh the rules and justify breaking the promise of confidentiality?

The appeal of the situational approach is that it reflects much of what we think when confronting this case. We take rules to be generally binding, but we also make room for exceptions. And we tend to make exceptions precisely when we think the consequences of breaking the rule will be good—or that keeping it will produce more harm than good. Thus, Fletcher's situational-utilitarian approach to ethics comes close to a commonsense, experiential, intuitive approach to moral decision making.

Consequences and Duty

The situational challenge puts all rules in jeopardy: rules are clearly tenuous if everything hinges on the good or bad results that can be brought about in any situation. And yet . . . most of us are not altogether comfortable with the suggestion that we should break the rule *any time* we think that we could do more good than harm by doing so.

This is because the situational approach reflects part—but only part—of our normal sense about what is right to do. No matter how good the consequences might be if we broke a promise, or how bad if we kept it, most of us probably feel some compunction about keeping a promise just because it has been made.

Suppose I have promised to pay the girl next door five dollars if she mows my lawn. Now perhaps she comes from a wealthy family, gets a good allowance, and does not need more money. Still, I suspect that most of us would cringe at the suggestion that I should then refuse to pay her on grounds that I can do more good with my money by giving it to a poor family up the street. Nor is it simply the bad consequences of breaking the promise—the child's disillusionment and hurt— that make us feel this way. There is something about making a promise that is more serious than that. Even though there might be good reasons for breaking the promise, we would feel some sense of guilt or anxiety about doing so.[19]

This reflects the fact that our morality is not simply a matter of calculating consequences. The nature of the human community is such that certain kinds of behavior are requisite to keep us human.[20] Among these are truth telling and keeping promises, without which we could never depend on anything or develop any sense of trust and covenant.

Morality is not simply a matter of weighing consequences, then. It is also a matter of adhering to the structural requisites for human community. If promise making is central to the nature of human community, and promise keeping is integral to the maintenance of that community as a *human* community, then the reasons for keeping promises do not depend entirely on the consequences of the individual case, nor even on the consequence in general. To break a promise is to act in a less than human manner to some extent, no matter how good the consequences. While exceptions to the rule can be found, they require serious reason, not just any balance of good over evil.

The rule that binds the minister to confidentiality is not totally dependent upon a calculation of consequences, then. In part, it reflects our deep sense of the structural requisites for human beings to live together. Promises are not to be broken lightly, nor simply when we think that more good than harm would come. Promise keeping is a *duty* as well as a calculated risk of balancing good and bad consequences. There is a deontological as well as a teleological element here. It is this element that appears to be missing from the situational approach that focuses so exclusively on the consequences of action.[21]

Situations and Rules

But morality is not a question of choosing rules over situations, or consequences over duty. As James Gustafson charges, to see the issue this way is to stage a "misplaced" debate.[22] Both situations *and* rules are involved in every ethical decision.

Indeed, Fletcher acknowledges one absolute rule—the rule of maximizing good consequences. Thus, his situational approach is not as free from rules as it seems.

More important, the situational approach rests on a questionable view of rules. Fletcher sees rules as absolutes that ignore the particularity of situations. But this is not the case. All rules—or norms—are written *for* situations. "Responsible parenthood" is a norm that applies only to those involved in or contemplating parenthood. "Keep promises" applies only to those who have made promises. Every rule or norm is written about and directed to situations. The rule of professional confidentiality is limited to professionals in professional settings. Thus, there is always a situation built into the very definition of a rule.

The crucial question, therefore, is not whether the situation matters, or whether we shall have rules or only situations, but what the situation is, how it is defined, and what rules are appropriately understood to apply to that situation. If the situation is defined as one in which professionals and clients are dealing with each other, then the rules that govern professional–client relations will apply. Situations are never independent of rules, nor are rules independent of situations.

Fletcher's complaint may legitimately be that the situation has been defined too broadly, and that morally relevant aspects of it are ignored in such a broad sweep. A general rule such as "never tell a lie" seems to ignore important differences between situations. This is a legitimate criticism to bring to some definitions of rules. But then, the quarrel is not with the existence of rules, but with the breadth they are given. The question is not whether we should follow rules, but whether the rules have been well written.

The rule of professional confidentiality is broadly drafted—e.g., "should *never* be divulged without consent." Such a drafting ignores possible justifiable exceptions, such as contemplated harm to another person.[23] The real question here is whether there are aspects of this case that would constitute justifiable exceptions to the general rule or would make us want to draft the rule more narrowly—e.g., "should never be divulged *except* in circumstances A, B, and C."

Just as rules are never independent of situations, so situations are never independent of rules, or of the moral notions that underlie them. Suppose a woman in a Nazi prison camp knows that she will be released if she becomes pregnant. Would it be wrong for her to commit adultery in order to secure her release and be returned to her family? Fletcher argues that it would not be wrong. Hence, the rule against adultery does not hold and no rules are absolutely binding.

Yet even in describing this situation and arguing that adultery is not wrong, Fletcher is forced to make use of moral notions. *Adultery* is not a value-free term. It is a concept that depends on a certain understanding of what is normally acceptable in married relations. To define the situation as one in which adultery is involved is to draw on those moral notions. We cannot define situations without using such moral notions.[24]

Norms and situations are not independent, then. Rules take situations seriously and definitions of situations already incorporate moral notions. The rule "keep promises" applies only to certain situations. Similarly, when we look at a situation, we lift up certain aspects of it as crucial for our moral decision making. We *define* the situation in certain ways, and these already begin to suggest the norms that are applicable. The issue is not whether we should follow rules or follow the demands of the situation, but how we are to understand the crucial aspects of the situation and the rules that are brought into play by them.

Prima Facie Duties

Is there some way to appreciate the important aspects of a situation without losing the value that we gain from rules?

I think so. A distinction introduced by W. D. Ross between "prima facie" duties and "duty proper" may provide the key.[25] This distinction provides grounds for holding that certain acts tend to be right because of the nature of the act that they are; these are prima facie duties. Yet in a given circumstance, our actual duty or duty proper might be something else. In such a system, there are no absolute rules of the kind that Fletcher deplores. Yet there is something other than merely consequences, for the nature of the act counts as well.

Ross locates seven prima facie duties. Those based on prior acts of my own include (1) making reparation for wrongs done, and (2) keeping promises. Those based on the prior act of another are (3) duties of gratitude. (4) Doing good (beneficence) and (5) avoiding evil (non-maleficence) are general duties, as is (6) the duty of justice or equitable distribution of goods and evils. Finally, there is (7) a duty of self-improvement (in virtue and intelligence). To this list, we might add (8) respect for the liberty and self-determination of the other (sometimes called the duty of autonomy, sometimes the principle of respect for persons), and (9) truth telling. There may be others as well. Such rules express in broad terms the structural requisites for human community.

An act will *tend* to be right insofar as it matches one of these prima facie duties. Hence, an act of gratitude is always prima facie right, and an act of ingratitude is always prima facie wrong. In each case where our act fits a prima facie duty, we can start with a presumption that the act is right. Justification for doing something else requires demonstrating that this prima facie rightness can be overridden.[26]

However, an act may not be right even though it is an act of promise keeping or matches some other prima facie duty. Most acts, if carefully described, can be seen to intersect with several prima facie duties: as I keep confidence, I am also harming someone. Thus, my duty proper or actual duty in the situation is calculated by assessing *all* of the respects in which the act may be judged to be required or prohibited by any of the prima facie duties.

Weighing Duties

This approach to moral decision making does not establish absolute rules that cannot be overridden. Nor does it leave everything to a calculation of consequences. Consequences will count, since there are always the prima facie duties of beneficence and non-maleficence. But the actor makes a decision about the act by weighing not just the consequences, but all the prima facie duties that might be involved. These are not simply random or arbitrary, but reflect a moral consensus about the nature of acts. Hence, the rules are binding without being absolute. Any violation of the rule requires justification, but such justification is not impossible.

Moreover, we have some guidelines for what constitutes sufficient justification: only when the act simultaneously fulfills one prima facie duty and violates another is there reason to refuse it as our duty proper. This means that not just any reason will do, but only those reasons that relate to prima facie duties. In considering whether to break a promise, Ruth must consider what other prima facie duties are involved and whether any of them are sufficient to override the duty of promise keeping.

Ross gave no absolute guidelines for balancing prima facie duties. An intuitionist, he believed that the binding quality of the various prima facie duties involved would be intuited in the moment. The desire to do good is not always the most binding or determining factor. Ross held that non-maleficence and promise keeping were probably more binding in most circumstances than are the other prima facie duties. However, he recognized that much would depend on the nature of the situation (e.g., the strength of the promise made, or the nature of the good to be done by breaking it), and so trusted the intuition of rational persons to determine the actual duty in the situation.[27]

To some, this system of balancing prima facie duties may not be very satisfactory. It would certainly be easier to have clear and absolute rules for what to do. However, this is not the way reality is, nor is it the way we actually think morality works. We can all think of cases where we thought a promise should be broken, and of other instances in which we were appalled that one was broken, even though the person did so for the best of motives.

In short, this approach accords with much of our actual decision making. It helps to explain why we feel uneasy about breaking a promise even when we think we are justified in doing so. Our uneasiness comes from the fact that we have broken a prima facie duty (even as we fulfilled another). It helps explain why even the good consequences that might come from a failure to tell the truth or keep a promise do not always seem to us to justify the lie or breach of confidence.

Morally Relevant Factors

Perhaps most important, this approach begins to answer a question left dangling by the situational approach: Which aspects of the situation count? The strength of the situational approach lies in its recognition of the fact that not all situations are alike. Indeed, no two situations are exactly alike, for each contains people with distinct histories. Nonetheless, not all aspects of a situation are morally relevant or should make a difference in the outcome. For example, the fact that one person has brown eyes and the other has blue eyes should not change the decision about what is right for each to do. Yet most situationists offer few guidelines as to which aspects of the situation should make a difference and which should not. If justice requires that we treat similar cases similarly, how do we decide which cases are sufficiently similar so that they should be treated alike and which are sufficiently different so that a different moral judgment is justified?[28]

This is what ethicists call "morally relevant differences." Application of this notion keeps decisions from being arbitrary. I cannot claim exemption from moral requirements simply because my situation differs from yours. I must show in what ways it differs, and I must show why those differences are relevant.[29] Much of our history consists of arguments and redefinitions of what factors count as morally relevant. Where we once thought that skin color and sex were relevant differences that justified unequal or dissimilar treatment of people, we no longer do. It becomes crucial, then, to know what kinds of things are morally relevant and justify changing our moral judgment.

This is where I believe Ross's concept of prima facie duties may be most helpful. The aspects of a situation that are morally relevant—and hence, those that justify a different moral decision—are those that have some direct bearing on one or another of the prima facie duties. An explicit or implicit promise is morally relevant because of the prima facie duty of promise keeping. Any action taken will have to be judged in part in accord with whether it violates or upholds this prima facie duty. In this case, the relevance of the factor, and its relation to the prima facie duties, is quite clear and obvious.

Sometimes the link is not so clear, and it is necessary to establish a relation between the aspect of the situation and some prima facie duty. For example, is the fact that Kathy cannot pay for an abortion morally relevant? Suppose she would have to use her parents' medical insurance to secure an abortion. If so, then Kathy's parents will be implicated, at least financially, in Kathy's actions. They are involved, whether or not Kathy wants them to be. If the parents' involvement and claims are not considered, they are not being treated fairly. If they do not receive information important to their own decision making in something that involves them, they are not being honored as moral agents. In short, because of the financial circumstances of the case, two additional prima facie duties come into play for Ruth: justice and respect for persons.

Morally relevant factors in a situation, then, are those factors that bear directly or indirectly on the fulfillment of prima facie duties. It is these factors that make a difference in deciding what to do. While sorting out the morally relevant factors does not give automatic answers, and there are no hard and fast rules for action, we do get a system of moral analysis that begins to highlight some aspects of the situation more than others. We begin to see which factors count in Ruth's situation, and how they might make a difference in her decision about what to do.

Discernment

To sort out which factors in a situation are morally relevant requires a faculty of discernment.[30] Acting ethically is not simply a matter of following rules or calculating consequences. It is also a matter of discerning which rules are called into play in the situation, and which aspects of the situation might change the way we balance or apply those rules. Only when we perceive correctly that a promise has been made, or that the action contemplated will affect other parties in a certain way, do we begin to know that the prima facie duties of promise keeping, respect for persons, and justice are involved. To act ethically, therefore, we need to develop a capacity for discernment.

In his discussion of this capacity, James Gustafson suggests that the quality of discernment or discrimination points to "the ability to distinguish the important from the unimportant information and the insightful interpretations from the uninsightful."[31] This is much the same as the ability to distinguish morally relevant differences. However, it also includes an interpretive capacity that requires imagination: "It refers to the ability to suggest inferences that can be drawn from the information, and thus to an imaginative capacity."[32] The task is not simply to locate important aspects of the situation, but to see *why* they are important, and what they suggest about possible resolution.

Several clergy, for example, have noted that Kathy's description of her situation involves two patterns of parent-child murder: her declaration that "my parents would kill me" and her own decision to abort her child.[33] This suggests that the daughter is more her parents' child than she may realize! Such an interpretation of the situation seems to me to demonstrate the quality of moral discernment—perceiving significant patterns that need to be lifted up in order for the moral meaning of the action to be made clear.

Summing Up

We began with the difficult question of whether a minister can break confidence. We saw that she is bound to a rule that requires her to keep confidence, and that there are good reasons for that rule. We also raised the question whether

29

there are aspects of the situation that might justify breaking the rule in this case. Using Ross's system of prima facie duties, we suggested a way of lifting up certain aspects of the situation as morally relevant or sufficient to change the moral decision. And then, finally, we argued that a quality of discernment is necessary to perceive these morally relevant aspects of the situation.

Clearly, then, moral decisions are never simply a question of rules or situations, but have a great deal to do with the perspective of the person who must discern what is important. At the same time, we are not left with a totally subjective approach: discernment is discernment *of* something that exists *in* the situation that *relates* to prima facie duties and their fulfillment. Hence, moral decision making is always an interplay between the act of discernment, the actual situation, and certain general moral duties.

We turn now to see whether it makes a difference for the person to be a professional and the situation to occur in a professional setting. Are there special rules for professionals, or are professionals bound only by the general prima facie duties? This is the question with which we begin chapter 2.

2. ROLES
AND MORALITY

CERTAIN aspects of a situation make a difference in our moral judgments. Salient features of the situation are those which activate prima facie duties or affect how we would balance the duties at stake. These are morally relevant aspects of the situation.

But now a crucial question arises. Does it make a difference to be in a professional setting or role? Is Ruth's dilemma about keeping confidence any different because of her position as a minister than it would be if she had been sought out simply as a friend? Is the professional role a morally relevant feature of the situation that should change the outcome of the decision?

This was the issue at stake several years ago when Robert Veatch argued that there is no special "professional ethics."[1] In the case precipitating his pronouncement, a group of physicians had decided not to tell the truth to a dying patient. They claimed that their medical oath *primum non nocere*, "first of all, do no harm," bound them to avoid doing anything that might harm the patient—including divulging upsetting information. Though they upheld the general principle of truth telling and would have abhorred lying in most circumstances, they did not feel bound to disclose harmful information to patients. Thus, they either seemed to think that the general prima facie duty did not apply to them in their professional role, or that it was overridden by a role-specific obligation that was more stringent and justified exemption from the prima facie duty.

Can physicians claim that their situation differs simply *because* they are physicians? Does the fact of professional

31

status or role constitute a morally relevant difference in the situation?

Veatch rejected the notion of a professional ethic that exempts practitioners from adhering to generally accepted ethical principles. Some duties are arduous and some ethical dilemmas painful. To permit professional groups exemption from normal rules opens the way to all sorts of special pleading and excuse making. How tempting it is to say, "I'm a professional. Rules that apply to other people don't necessarily apply to me. I can decide whether to tell the truth as I please." It is this special pleading that Veatch eschewed. He argued correctly that professionals are not necessarily experts in moral judgment and should not be permitted to hide behind some concept of "professionalism" in order to avoid difficult moral decisions or painful ethical principles. In so doing, he rejected the notion that being a professional, or being in a professional role when a dilemma arises, is itself a morally relevant feature of the situation.

But I suspect that the physicians involved in Veatch's case would not have thought that they were exempt from any moral duties. Rather, they would have argued that they were held to an even more stringent (or higher) set of duties.[2] Most professional groups develop codes that proscribe some behaviors and prescribe others.[3] In places where a layperson might justifiably break confidence or fail to offer assistance, the professional may be bound by the code to keep confidence or give assistance even at great personal risk, such as going to jail. Physicians, lawyers, and ministers all work under strict requirements of confidentiality. Priests must stop at the scene of any accident—no matter what prior commitments they have made to be somewhere. To belong to a profession is traditionally to be held to certain standards of conduct that go beyond the norm for others. As occupational groups struggle to gain professional status and recognition, a common step in the process is the development and adoption of a strict code of ethics governing and delimiting behavior.[4]

The physicians who argued that they need not tell the truth to a dying patient were thus not simply trying to squeeze out of a difficult situation. They were adhering—rightly or wrongly—to what they understood as a special and stringent requirement for medical practitioners: *primum non nocere,* "first of all, do no harm."[5] In their view, they were justified in breaking the principle of truth telling because they were bound to an even more stringent requirement not to harm. The exemption from one principle is balanced by the assumption of other duties arising from the professional role. In this case, their professional position activated the prima facie duty of non-maleficence, and made it particularly heavy.

Roles and Behavior

The nature of much morality is this: roles exempt us from some duties but impose others. Parents of small children may be exempted from jury duty in order to fulfill their child-rearing expectations. The normal duties of citizenship are waived so that they may fulfill the special duties that go with raising children. The balance of obligations is justified on the assumption that those special duties are of vital interest to the state.

Similarly, the classic "sick role" brings with it a delicate balancing of exemption from normal duties and assumption of new duties: the patient may stay home from work or renege on social obligations, but in exchange is expected to seek medical advice and make a genuine effort to get well.[6] It will not do to go to the ball game instead of staying in bed! Thus, some normal duties may be ignored, but only because there are special duties that attach to the role of sick person.

Everyday morality is closely bound to roles. "*As a teacher,* I must do Y or Z." "I have to attend the school play; I'm her *mother.*" "*As a minister,* I cannot break confidence." As Dorothy Emmet puts it, a person "in deciding what . . . to do, . . . will be likely to take into account, even if only to reject, notions of what is expected, e.g., of a son."[7] We think about our obligations in terms of our roles.

And so professionals, too, might be exempted from some normal duties—but only at the price of assuming additional

33

duties or special duties that go with the role. In order to clarify this exchange of expectations and its implications for professional ethics, we must examine the concept of a role.

The term *role* reminds us of a play or drama, in which we might take on a character for a specified time. To many people, the notion of playing a role has negative connotations—it suggests that the person is not being quite "real" in some way, but is "play acting." This is an understandable reaction, and it may account for some of our negative associations with the idea of professional roles and the suggestion that they would be important in morality.[8]

But our everyday lives are full of roles. There is no way to live without assuming several roles. A role is a capacity in which we act toward others.[9] It indicates how we act in a structured situation. As Edwin Lemert explains: "A situation is structured to the degree that others with whom the individual interacts expect him to respond in certain ways and to the extent that he anticipates their expectations and incorporates them into his behavior."[10] In short, social situations become structured as patterns of interaction develop and certain behaviors are expected. Where these are of a recognizable type, people begin to be identified with and to identify themselves by those structured expectations or capacities: "She's my friend; he's a teacher; I'm a firefighter."

Some of these structures or capacities are occupationally defined: minister, surgeon, police officer. Some are not occupationally related: lover, daughter, enemy. Some roles seem to cross boundaries between occupational and non-occupational capacities: "mother" is primarily a relational (non-occupational) role, but it has become identified as an occupation as well—"I'm a housewife and mother." Since some roles are relational and some occupational, most of us play several roles at the same time: child, parent, citizen, and professional.

Identifying people by their roles is one of the ways we sort information in order to make sense out of our world. "What do you do?" is an inquiry about occupational role. It tells us something about who the person is and what kind of behavior is appropriate around this person. It also tells us what conversation we might profitably pursue. In a new situation, we often find it profitable to ask which person plays what role: "Who's in charge here?" Confusion results when roles are reversed from our assumptions or prejudices—e.g., when the middle-aged man is the secretary and the young woman is his boss.

Carried to an extreme, people lose their personal identities and become totally identified with their roles, either by themselves or by others. We all know teachers who never stop being "the teacher"—even when on a hike or at a birthday party. Ministers are often expected to be always in a ministerial role—available to listen and counsel and provide comfort.[11] The women's movement has surfaced the anger many women feel when they are totally identified with a role such as wife or mother to the exclusion of their personal identity.

Such a total identification with roles can be dangerous when it comes to ethics. The person may lose her or his ability to question the normal expectations that go with the role. We have come to expect politicians to lie, but that does not make it right! A politician who identifies totally with the role will lose her or his ability to step back and examine the ethical requirements of the situation. Indeed, we get our caricatures of professional groups—the stealthy lawyer, the overly pious minister—from taking to extremes the normal role morality of those groups.

All of this suggests that roles have built into them some notion of typical behavior associated with the role. Teenagers who follow rock stars become "groupies." They are expected to scream themselves hoarse and throw themselves on the stage. When others exhibit the same behavior, we label them "groupies" as well. This helps us to know what to expect—and what not to expect—of them. In short, we come to recognize certain types of behavior as belonging to a role and we expect (though we do not always approve!) that behavior from those in the role. Mothers are not expected to behave as groupies do. Although it would be possible for someone to be both a mother and a groupie, the expectations normally attached to those roles are mutually incompatible. As Emmet suggests, "A role relation in a social situation has some notion of conduct as appropriate or inappropriate built into its description."[12]

This is another way of saying that the notion of a role has *normative* content. It suggests that certain behavior ought or ought not to be done by someone in that role. Suppose R is rushed to the emergency room with a knife wound. P and Q are standing by. What should they do? Until we know what their roles are, we have no idea how to answer this question. As soon as we learn that P is a nurse and Q is a minister, we form a picture of what behavior would be appropriate for each of them: one is to administer medical aid; the other is to pray or administer sacraments.

The mere identification of roles thus suggests the existence and application of certain norms: "You have to help him; he's your brother." "No minister should have made *that* mistake." Because the concept of a role has built into it some expectations of proper behavior, roles provide a link between factual statements about what the situation is and normative assumptions about what the actors ought to do. To ask what roles are involved in a situation is implicitly to ask something about the behavior that would be appropriate or inappropriate in that situation. What should one do when R is rushed into the emergency room? Much depends on whether one is P or Q. Some things are right or wrong to do simply because one is in a particular role. Roles provide an initial link between the definition of the situation and the determination of what ought to be done.[13]

Everyday morality is thus not simply a matter of rules or of situations. It is also a matter of roles. Does it make a difference to encounter an ethical dilemma in a professional setting? It does if the role of professional brings with it some expectations about behavior that differ from the expectations we would otherwise have. Roles are not the whole of morality, for role expectations can be wrong. But they do provide a beginning point.

Role Morality and General Obligations

How strong are role expectations? How do we balance them against general ethical principles and prima facie obligations? Let us return to Veatch's case of the doctors who lied to a dying patient, and then to our own case of Ruth's struggle with the question of confidentiality.

Although Veatch argues that there is no special professional ethics that would exempt doctors from normal prima facie duties, he does acknowledge that there may be particular obligations that apply to persons in certain kinds of roles. For example, professional persons have debts to their mentors for teaching them the profession. The duty of gratitude may therefore apply to their situation.[14]

But gratitude is a universal norm, or prima facie duty. It does not exist *only* for professionals. It applies to anyone who has been the recipient of services or gifts. Thus, if it applies to professionals, that is because they have received gifts. Laypeople who have received gifts should also be grateful. There is no special norm for professionals, but only a question about the situation—whether or not one has received gifts. This morally relevant factor activates a general norm and brings it into play. When I accept the services of my teachers, or the training given to me in a field education setting in a church, I implicitly take on an obligation of gratitude to those teachers and supervisors.

It is these concrete actions and exchanges between people, Veatch claims, that create particular obligations or change the situation for professionals. There is no special professional ethics or rules that apply to professionals and not to others, but only factors in the situation that activate certain prima facie duties. Bayles would call these duties of professionals "specifications" of ordinary rules.[15]

In order to justify the application of different norms, then, professionals should be able to point to such morally relevant factors. It is not enough to point to the status of being a professional. Saying "I'm a physician"—as the physicians in this case seemed to want to do—is not sufficient. If professionals want to claim exemption from certain ethical judgments or norms, they must show the ground for such exemption in the specific promises and commitments that constitute morally relevant differences of their situation. In the case at hand, Veatch does not consider the implicit commitment to care for the patient to be sufficient justification for failing to abide by the prima facie duty of truth telling. There is, in his judgment, no specific exchange or action that justifies exemption from the duty to tell the truth.

In contrast to Veatch, Kenneth Kipnis argues that there need not be specific actions or exchanges to establish special duties or exemptions for professionals.[16] He suggests that social positions themselves *can* be morally relevant and sufficient to alter normal obligations. For example, parents have special rights and responsibilities that are properly taken into account when deciding what they should do. Parents must provide adequately for the health and education of their children, and may not abandon them on the street. These responsibilities do not apply to others. Yet no specific promises have been made to anyone. The mere fact of being a parent makes the difference. The role relationship itself is morally relevant. There can be special rules for persons in certain social positions.[17] There might, then, be special rules applying to professionals simply as professionals, and not necessarily because of specific exchanges or commitments.

What is at stake in this argument is whether there is a morally relevant difference that arises from the mere fact of occupying a social role, or whether the social role is to be taken simply as a clue to specific prior commitments and special agreements that might be morally relevant. If we take Veatch's position, then the justification for violation of any prima facie duty requires the ability to locate the specific actions or agreements that are morally relevant. For example, Ruth could not depend on her professional code to justify keeping confidence, but must point to her specific promise to do so. If we take Kipnis's position, then the justification for breaking rules seemingly does not require such a stringent standard of locating specific agreements, but requires only that we can point to a socially recognized role or status. Ruth could claim a duty to keep confidence based solely on her profession and the expectations that attach to it.

In my opinion, these arguments are not mutually exclusive. A full picture of morally relevant differences includes both specific actions and general considerations of role. Specific promises or exchanges, whether explicit or implicit, certainly do make a difference. If I have promised to give Smith half my lottery winnings, and you have made no such promise, then our situations are clearly different if one of us wins the lottery. I have an obligation to pay Smith, while you do not. Many of the obligations that attach to particular roles can be traced to such implicit or explicit commitments. When a lawyer accepts a client, or a minister agrees to a counseling session with a parishioner, that lawyer or minister can be said to have taken a specific action that brings with it special commitments and promises, such as the commitment to confidentiality. These are clearly morally relevant for determining what ought to be done.

At the same time, the content of those special commitments and promises is defined at least in part by general expectations of what lawyers and ministers are supposed to do. It is part of the social definition of the role that lawyers and ministers keep secrets confidential. Clients and parishioners expect to share in confidence even when nothing explicit is said about confidentiality. If Kathy had seen Ruth in a coffee shop and had sat down and blurted out her problem in that setting, she would nonetheless expect Ruth to keep confidence. A role relationship is an entire complex of expectations and obligations that cannot simply be confined to a set of prior acts or commitments. The specific acts or commitments to which Veatch points are supplemented and given shape by the social definition of the role.

Indeed, neither our roles nor the obligations that go with them are always chosen willingly or knowingly. We are born into family relationships. Though we may not choose to be a daughter or a son, we nonetheless have obligations to honor our parents. Some people have not chosen to bear children, but find themselves parents through contraceptive failure or forced intercourse or rape. The fact that they have not chosen the role of parent does not necessarily exempt them from fulfilling the obligations that go with that role.[18]

Thus, role obligations cannot always be linked to a specific prior action taken by the role-holder. All of us can think of a time when someone has turned us into a confidant in circumstances where we did not invite the sharing of secrets and would rather not have known the specific information. Nonetheless, the sharing of information puts us in the role of confidant—at least in the other person's eyes—whether or not we welcome it.

Hence, we can agree with Veatch that being in a special role or professional position does not exempt the person from general ethical principles or prima facie duties that apply to all people. Yet we can also acknowledge a host of additional obligations that may be brought to bear by the role. Some of these will be present because of specific commitments and exchanges. Some are simply the application of prima facie duties in a specific context. But others arise out of the entire complex of expectations and assumptions that are generally defined for the role.

There is a sense, then, in which simply being in a particular position *may* change the situation in relevant ways. Doctors or ministers may not be in the same position as anyone else when it comes to telling the truth or keeping confidence. There may in fact be a professional difference. This difference is formed in part by the specific commitments and prior acts of the professional and in part by the social ethos surrounding the role definition of those professions. As Chris Hackler suggests, the general rules governing professional conduct may be the same as the rules governing anyone else's conduct.[19] However, they are activated or not depending on the social role. Norms are universal in the sense that there are no special norms for particular groups, yet relevant differences between groups can change the way the norm is applied and the times when it is activated. "Keep promises" is a norm that applies in general—it is a prima facie duty. But it is given shape for professional groups in very specific obligations to keep confidence.

A Test Case

Let us return to the case of Ruth and Kathy in order to see how these considerations might help us determine what to do. Does Ruth's professional role make a difference? I will argue that it does—and most of the ministers with whom I have shared this case have also argued that it does.

The issue is keeping confidence. The minister is approached in her office and a specific request for confidence is made. Is there anything about the setting or the role that binds the minister more stringently than someone else might be bound?

Of course, in our case study, Ruth gives an explicit promise of confidentiality. She gives assurance that anything shared with her will not go beyond the walls of the office. Thus, she has made one of Veatch's concrete agreements. This is morally relevant, and it does bind her more stringently than if she had not.

But what if she had not given this promise? Suppose Kathy had simply walked into the office, burst into tears, and disclosed her predicament. Would there be anything specially binding in that circumstance? No explicit promise has been made. Does this mean that the obligation to keep confidence is less stringent?

Most ministers answered no to this question. "It doesn't matter whether she made an explicit promise. She's in her office, and the parishioner should expect confidence." "She's still a minister, after all." "It wouldn't matter where it happened. As long as she knows the young woman because of her work in the church, she's in the ministerial role." These are the kinds of responses the question evokes.

What these responses suggest is that there is something about being in the professional role that brings with it a stringent obligation no matter what the other circumstances

41

are. Some thought the role was reinforced by the fact that the encounter took place in the office; but most agreed that even if it had happened over a cup of coffee in the local café, the minister would still be bound to confidentiality *as a part of the expectations of her role.* Some pointed to the existence of codes of professional ethics that require confidentiality of ministers, but many were unaware whether they had such a code and what it required. Even in the absence of a specific code, their feeling was that ministers *must* keep confidence even in difficult situations. "I wouldn't tell anybody else unless I could get her permission to." "I would try to get her to tell her parents. But no, if she refused, I wouldn't tell them without her permission."

In short, the role of minister seems to bring with it, either explicitly in its professional codes or implicitly in the understanding that ministers and others bring to the role, a stringent obligation to keep confidence. It might be permissible for others to break confidence—for example, a friend or boyfriend might justifiably break confidence. But the minister is bound to keep confidence. Indeed, the literature written by ministers often sees it as an absolute requirement: "Under no circumstances will a minister betray a confidence."[20] "No word should ever escape his lips."[21] "Pastoral interviews and everything relating to them are to be kept absolutely secret."[22] For ministers, it seems, confidentiality or promise keeping is not simply one prima facie duty among others; it has a special place. It is what Bayles calls a functional (or role-activated) duty.

However, this does not solve all the problems related to this case and to justifying what one ought to do. Some were uncomfortable with Ruth's position because she was an associate minister, and they thought she ought to inform her senior colleague. Others pointed out that she has obligations to Kathy's parents as well as to Kathy. While the requirement to keep confidentiality appears to be a major requirement of the role obligations of ministers, it is not the only requirement. As one minister put it, "My basic obligation is to work for wholeness and healing. I have to do whatever will best bring about healing in this circumstance." Confidentiality is not the *only* role-activated obligation for ministers. Before we can decide what ought to be done, we need also to look at what our role obligations are, and where they come from. It is to this task that we turn in chapter 3.

3. EXPECTATIONS AND OBLIGATIONS: ROLES IN ACTION

IT seems that being in a professional role is a morally relevant difference that changes our assessment of what to do in a situation. This is because roles bring with them notions of what is expected. But how do role expectations arise? Who defines them? What causes a form of behavior to become associated with a role as right or appropriate for someone in the role? And when do role expectations become obligations?

The answers to these questions are not simple. Some expectations are spelled out in contracts—"The associate minister will develop a Christian education program." These are clearly obligatory. But most are not so explicit, nor do they clearly become obligations. Role expectations arise in a complicated interplay involving professions, society, and individual professionals.

The profession defines appropriate behavior to some extent—for example, ministers serve on examining boards to admit new members for ordination. Society at large also defines appropriate behavior to some extent. Laws give ministers immunity from prosecution when they refuse to divulge confidential information. Subtle mechanisms also operate. People shun the church of a minister thought to be too radical and assume that lewd jokes are not appropriate when ministers are present.

The individual role-holder also brings a particular style to the role. One minister is flamboyant and outgoing, another reserved and scholarly. Each establishes and influences the expectations that others will come to have of those in the role.

Role expectations change over time. Ministers were once expected to be the "learned ones" in the community—the best educated, most scholarly, most knowledgeable or book-read. Later, they were expected to be the most spiritual and exemplary in their sexual and ethical behavior.

In a fascinating study, Ann Douglas argues that the role of minister underwent a tremendous shift during the latter part of the nineteenth century—a shift toward an "interiorization" of values and a "feminization" of the role.[1] The image of minister as weak, effeminate, timid, gentle, and spiritual rather than physical derives from the shift in role experienced under the economic and social pressures of the day. Whether or not her characterization is entirely accurate, it is clear that the role of minister has undergone change and will continue to do so.[2] Part of what it means for a role to change is that expectations of behavior change.

Appropriate role behavior is shaped by many factors. I find four of these particularly helpful in establishing a framework for ethical analysis: aims, images, models, and professional training.

Aims of the Role

Roles are often defined around a central goal or aim. This goal then helps to determine what behavior is appropriate in the role. For example, parenthood is a role aimed at the rearing and training of children. As indicated in chapter 2, parents may be exempted from some duties of citizenship in order to fulfill the special duties of child-rearing that go with the role. These duties set limits on what parents may do. They may not abandon their children or neglect them. They must provide education and medical care. They are expected to set a context for the moral development of the child. They must feed and clothe their children. Some of these expectations are encoded into law. Others become a part of our implicit expectations of those in the role. Parents who violate these expectations are subject to censure—and in extreme cases, may have the role taken away from them. The aims of a role

45

thus have normative implications. They help to determine what is expected of those in the role, and set the stage for assessing obligations.[3]

Similarly, the purposes of a profession help to determine the role obligations of those within it. For example, medicine as a profession could be said to have as its overriding aim the physical health and well-being of the person.[4] Anything detrimental to that purpose will tend to be seen as a violation of the role and its expectations. The Hippocratic Oath's admonition not to "give to a woman a pessary to cause an abortion"[5] is an expression of a norm derived from this basic purpose, as is the maxim *primum non nocere*. What is chosen as the preeminent good or purpose of the professional group will set limits on appropriate role behavior.

What does this mean for ministry? Is there a preeminent good or overarching purpose that helps to determine appropriate role behavior? Several ministers responding to Ruth's case were uncomfortable about keeping confidence because of their assumption that they are *primarily* to work for the wholeness of the parishioner. They were expressing a sense that ministry has an overriding purpose, and that this purpose should help define what they are to do in the circumstance. Here, they took this purpose to be the integration of Kathy's life into a sense of meaning. Her spiritual as well as physical health was at stake, and it was their job to pay attention to the spiritual dimension. This suggests a view of the primary purpose of ministry as a shepherding of the holistic health of the other, and the setting of appropriate behavior in accord with this goal. This view is not unlike Samuel Southard's suggestion that the goal of pastoral authority is "to help a person accept and relate to the power of God redemptively."[6]

One might define the goal of ministry differently.[7] But the point is clear: in order to know what role expectations are appropriate within ministry, we need some understanding of the purposes of ministry. When a minister and congregation disagree about appropriate behavior, the argument may have to do with basic understandings of the goals and purposes of ministry. Not until these are discussed and clarified will there be agreement on the appropriate behavior for the clergy. For example, some argue that ministers should not be involved politically.[8] Participation in the civil rights struggle or in anti-war protest is considered inappropriate, for it violates the primary aim of spiritual assistance and shepherding the flock. Some ministers, however, argue that political activity is integral to spiritual care, or that the primary aim of the profession is not simply spiritual care.[9]

Definition of the basic purposes of ministry is a task that must be undertaken both denominationally and ecumenically. No definitive answer can be given here. Evidence suggests that there is considerable denominational variation, with some denominations stressing a priestly role that accords with a purpose of mediating God's grace or judgment, others stressing a pastoral role that accords with a purpose of embodying God's love, while still others stress the prophetic role and its link with God's liberating activity.[10] The purposes of the church and of ordained ministry will both be important in making this determination.

For our purposes, it is sufficient to note that the definition given to the aims of the profession overall will set some limits on the behavior appropriate within that professional role. The aims of the profession are the first clue to role expectations and obligations.

Images

In addition to the aims of a role, we acquire images of what it means to hold that role well. "A good mother is always there when her children come home from school." "A good preacher holds you spellbound." These statements suggest images of the ideal role-holder. They also help to establish role expectations: that mothers will not work outside the home, or that preachers must have a particular delivery style. Moral judgments begin to be formed about those who fail to live up to such expectations: "She's not a good mother." "He's a poor preacher."

Most professionals have an ideal image of themselves as selfless, dedicated, tireless, competent, humble, and a host of other role-related virtues. Such images are upheld as well by society and are sometimes perpetuated within the professional group. Both patients and physicians may reject the concept of socialized medicine because they believe that the good physician is always available, and an eight-hour day and a five-day work week violate this image. Denominational bodies may admonish ministers to be uncomplaining, giving, and sacrificing—or to ignore the everyday demands of low salaries and difficult working and living conditions.[11]

Such images of the good or ideal role-holder incorporate a number of elements. First, there are questions of *style,* such as formality or informality. Is it appropriate for ministers to be flamboyant? Many would think not. As Charles Smith notes in his delightful spoof, ministers are normally expected to have a sober and sedate style.[12] The emphasis on dress in ministry gives some indication of how important style can be. Clearly, the traditional view is that "one's clothes should be inconspicuous"[13] and that "much of a man's personality is revealed by the way he dresses."[14] Thus, Episcopal priest Patricia Park notes that her gold earrings became a source of controversy in her first parish.[15]

Images also incorporate notions of *function.* Which tasks are appropriate to the role, and which are not? To judge a woman not a good mother because she is not home when her children return from school is to incorporate into the image of the role a definition of tasks that belong to the role. These are certainly open to debate. Thus, as noted above, clergy and their congregations sometimes disagree about whether the good minister is politically active.

Images also suggest norms for *relationship* within roles. We often judge physicians to be wanting because of their lack of availability or distance from their patients. The good role-holder is often the one who implies, "I'm always here to help you; we're in this together." As William Hulme puts it, the congregation's conception of the minister is "a good Joe."[16] The good minister is a friend or pal, not a prophet.

Assumptions about the professional's *commitment* to the role relationship also form a part of the ideal image of the role. The study "Readiness for Ministry" by the Association of Theological Schools (ATS) showed that all denominations rank "fidelity to tasks and persons" high on the list of expectations for ministers.[17]

Such ideal images take shape in the life histories of exemplary professionals or role models. Who has not identified with Albert Schweitzer or Florence Nightingale at some time in his or her youth? Most professionals can point to a particular person who influenced them to seek a career in that profession—a grandparent, a famous man or woman, a campus chaplain. Behind the budding lawyer or doctor may be the story of a Clarence Darrow or a Tom Dooley. Behind the minister lies the story of Jesus.[18]

Such stories are an important part of the development of role expectations. Stories link disparate elements into a coherent whole. They create meaning out of the absurd and provide continuity in the midst of chaos. Joan Didion expresses eloquently the power of stories: "We tell ourselves stories in order to live. . . . We look for the sermon in the suicide. . . . We live entirely . . . by the imposition of a narrative line upon disparate images."[19] Stories that give meaning to professional and other roles are crucial for seeing how behavior fits the role. As our understanding of a role changes, the stories that buoyed that role begin to crumble; as new stories emerge, roles are redefined.

Paradigms and Models

Images and stories do not tell us directly what to do. They offer no clear-cut set of rules for behavior. But they do yield paradigms and models for interpreting the world around us and responding to it. The models or paradigms we choose as basic to professional life have implications for the meaning of the profession and for determining proper conduct in ethical dilemmas.

Robert Veatch offers four possible models for the physician-patient relationship.[20] Each one gives rise to different tendencies in the ethical area. In the "engineering" model, the physician is a technician presenting data but making no decisions for the patient. At the opposite end of the spectrum is the "priestly" model, in which the physician tells the patient what she or he should do, based on a paternalistic assessment of what is good for the patient.[21] In the first, the professional takes no part in ethical decision making per se. In the second, the professional makes all the decisions, including the ethical ones.

Veatch rejects both of these as inadequate in a pluralistic society.[22] This leaves two other possibilities. The "collegial" model suggests that the decision should be made jointly—professional and patient are pals, co-adventurers, sharing common goals and aims. While this model includes some of those elements of style and relationship that are central to the professional role, Veatch questions whether it is a realistic model in the long run: the gap in knowledge between professional and client is too great for them to be true equals in the decision. Hence, Veatch opts for a "contract" or "covenant" model instead. Similarly, Michael Bayles proposes a "fiduciary" model.[23] Such a model does not assume that physician and patient share common goals and values, but rather permits them to specify a set of complementary obligations and benefits. Since mutually acceptable limits must be negotiated on the basis of these complementary aims and purposes, the covenant model implies at a minimum basic norms of truth telling and keeping promises. Thus, the professional would neither eschew all ethical decisions nor impose a decision on the client, but would negotiate about the best course of action on the basis of sharing honestly the values and goals involved on both sides.

Applied to Ruth's situation, these models would have quite different implications for what she is to do. In the "engineering" paradigm, she would secure information for Kathy about available options but would offer no judgments as to the suitability of abortion or involvement of other parties. In the "priestly" model, she would decide what was best for Kathy and attempt to secure it—even at the cost of breaking confidence. On the "collegial" model, she would become Kathy's pal and offer to go through every step of the process with her. Using the "covenant" model, she would put forth her own values and goals alongside Kathy's, in hopes that they could clarify mutual expectations and obligations.

Whether one agrees with the choice of a covenant or fiduciary model, the basic point is sound. Each model carries different implications for what would constitute appropriate behavior for the professional. Should a doctor tell the truth to a dying patient? Should a minister break confidence? Much depends on whether the professional is acting on a "priestly" or a "covenant" model. New models for professional-client relationships are needed, as are new images of the professional person.

Some new models are emerging. Letty Russell proposes a "partnership" model that incorporates recognition of the autonomy of those being served but also includes "solidarity" with them—a combination of elements from both collegial and covenant models. Drawing on the notion of advent and the surprise of God's promises throughout history, she argues for a "calculated inefficiency" in which the minister makes room for others to grow and experience their own strengths. [24]

David Switzer suggests that the clown image provides a good model for ministry: the clown is a trained professional "whose professional acts grow out of his/her own humanity and his/her understanding of the humanity of others."[25] In this model, professional competence and growth are directly related to personal growth, since it is the humanity of the minister that is the foundation of professional acts. The minister should be a "living model of openness and clarity of personal communication and self-disclosure."[26] Both this and the "partnership" model differ considerably from early models of the "gentleman and scholar."[27]

51

Professional Training

Models and images, as well as an understanding of the aims of the profession, are communicated through a complicated process of socialization into a role or profession. Professional training is thus an important source of role expectations. During training, young professionals pick up the "inside" view of what it means to be a practicing professional in that role.

One of the most important aspects of professional socialization is access to role models—real persons who embody some of those ideal images and stories discussed above. The professional in training looks to established practitioners to gain a sense of what it means to be a member of the profession and what constitutes acceptable or normative behavior in the profession. It is partly for this reason that women and members of minority groups deplore their lack of appropriate role models on professional school faculties and in "field education" settings.[28] Established women and minority persons are needed in the professions to give a sense of what it means to be there as a woman or minority person. The opportunity to live and work with colleagues in the field is an important source of the development of norms for proper behavior in the role.

Indeed, the desire to enter a profession is often linked to significant encounters with such role models. Many seminary students choose ministry because of the model set in their own home—and many still hold their own mothers or fathers as the ideal role model whom they try to emulate. Professional role models are the embodiments of the images, aims, and stories that help define the meaning of professional roles. It is for this reason that we often (erroneously) assume that professions run in families.

Professional training and education also inculcate values and ways of thinking that are peculiar to the profession. Each professional group develops a characteristic stance toward the world, a language with which to interpret it and respond to it. This stance carries normative implications. In *Whatever*

Became of Sin?, Karl Menninger deplores the shift from the language of theology to the language of medicine to describe and define the world.[29] When the inability to sustain relationships is seen as a "sickness" rather than a "sin," a different panoply of responses is evoked. These different world views do have normative implications. Their importance can hardly be overestimated, and we shall return to this issue in part III.

Such world views or stances are inculcated during professional training and education. Wendy Carlton documents the changes that occur as medical students proceed through their training.[30] Structures in the work setting reinforce certain ways of approaching problems and diminish other responses. By the third year, most medical students have lost their romantic, humanitarian ideals and have adopted a "professional" stance—a scientific mode of approach to patients and their problems. Students do not simply acquire new skills during professional training. They also learn new values. Where once they might have said that compassion was the most important ingredient in medical practice, by the third year most have come to value technical competence or diagnostic acuity as the most important ingredient. Similarly, Charles Bosk demonstrates the process by which systems of reward and punishment reinforce the maintenance of hierarchical lines of authority.[31]

Professional training thus helps determine the rules for professional behavior by providing a new language with which to interpret chaos, by showing role models in action, and by inculcating new values associated with the professional stance.

Some thirty years ago, H. Richard Niebuhr pointed to the confusion in theological schools over the image of ministry and hence its proper training.[32] Recent studies suggest that ministerial training remains in some turmoil and that there is a gap between training and actual demands of parish ministry.[33] Changes in theological education reflect changes taking place in the role of minister and suggest an implicit if not explicit recognition that new models and hence behavioral expectations are needed.

These four factors, then, help set the stage for determining appropriate role behavior. The aims of the profession establish initial presumptions and some boundaries around behavior. Images and stories of heroes and heroines within the profession give the ideal standards for behavior. Models have normative implication. Professional training provides the process by which these are incorporated into the practicing professional's own sense of self and work. All four depend on an interplay between the professional group and society at large. Each is partially responsible for setting the aims of the profession, deciding which practitioners shall be lifted up as heroes, and determining the structures within which professional training takes place.

Expectations and Conflicts

Given the variety of sources of role definition, it is no wonder role expectations are sometimes ambiguous or contradictory. The "good" pastor is always available to those in need, but the "good" preacher delivers a powerful sermon on Sunday morning. When sermon preparation time is interrupted by a parishioner in need, what should the minister do? Should she postpone the counseling session so as to finish the sermon, or drop the sermon to respond to the needs of the moment, risking the delivery of a "half-baked" sermon on Sunday?[34] Two different role expectations come into conflict here, each based on an image of the good minister held by pastor and parish alike.

Role expectations sometimes conflict directly like this. But sometimes they are simply unclear.[35] Is the good minister reserved and dignified (never laughing at dirty jokes) or warm and sociable (hugging parishioners and welcoming an invitation for a beer)? Role expectations are not always sufficiently clear to engender outright conflict. They may simply be ambiguous. This is particularly true for young people stepping into a post formerly held by an older, esteemed colleague. Must I be like my predecessor and do things the way he or she did? Or should I be different, having my own style? It is also particularly true for women and members of minority groups stepping into posts or professions formerly held by white males. As Helene Pollock puts it, "The pastor is supposed to 'act like a pastor,' but nobody spells out how a pastor is supposed to act, or exactly what a pastor is supposed to do."[36]

Role ambiguity and conflict arise from many sources. Most professionals play several roles within their professional work. The preacher is also pastor. The professor does administrative work as well as classroom teaching. Each sub-role within the profession has its own role expectations, and these are not always mutually compatible.

Each professional also has a set of nonprofessional roles: citizen, parent, child, friend, and client to other professionals. Expectations derived from these other roles can conflict with expectations of the professional role.[37] Many ministers struggle with their duties as spouses and parents in view of the seemingly endless demands of parishioners. Simply finding the day off to be with the family may be a serious problem in role conflict.[38] This is in part because the image of the good minister is one who is *always* available. Even when the written contract specifies time off, the implicit role expectations may create tension for the minister who unplugs the phone for a day. Recriminations and guilt feelings are not uncommon.

Other possibilities for conflict arise from the structures in which professionals work. These will be examined in more detail in part III. Here, it is important to note that ambiguity and conflict can arise not only from external sources such as expectations of different groups served, but also from internal sources. Ministers may differ with their congregations or denominational adjudicatories about their models for ministry and attendant obligations.[39] But they may also experience internal conflict.

A lighthearted illustration helps to make the point. As a child, I was deeply influenced by the stories of Sherlock Holmes. I fancied myself a steely-minded sleuth, dedicated to the task, eschewing emotion in favor of reason. Yet I was also taken by the stories of Winnie-the-Pooh. A Bear of Very Little Brain, Pooh is ruled by the stomach, not the head. He seems the very antithesis of Sherlock Holmes. Can both serve as models?

Now surely no professional models her life directly on either of these fictional characters. Yet many find themselves in a bind well represented by Pooh and Holmes—torn between their desire to be lovable souls and their sense that competent professional life requires rejection of emotion and dedication to objectivity. Indeed, congregations that expect a "good Joe" (or Jane) hold up a Pooh image, while denominations that expect a "promoter" hold up more of a Holmes image.[40] Few can manage to be both—indeed, the characters of Rabbit and Watson in the Pooh and Holmes stories imply that feeling and rational organization are incompatible modes of approach to the world. A balance must be struck.

However the balance is struck, clarity is needed before we can decide what to do in the situation. Role ambiguity and role conflict have debilitating effects on the role-holder.[41] Given sufficient unclarity, one reaches an ethical impasse. Are all expectations obligatory? How is one to choose when they conflict?

Take Ruth's case, for example. Should Ruth break confidence? The answer to this question depends in part on how she understands her role. Ruth may see her primary role responsibility as seeking Kathy's total well-being. Members of the congregation might think that her primary role responsibility is supporting family relationships. "After all," they might argue, "it's the adults who hire you, and they expect you not to permit adolescents to go against their parents." Each of these interpretations of primary role responsibility might yield a different perspective on the meaning of keeping confidence. In order to decide what to do, Ruth needs role clarity. Difficult though it may be to achieve such clarity, it could make all the difference in the world for solving her ethical dilemma.

Summary: Roles and Morality

The importance of role clarity is well illustrated by a recent case involving role conflict for a medical student who proposed to turn sociologist and observe the work of a nontraditional healer.[42]

The question arose: What should the student do if he thought the patient was being harmed by the healer? As a *medical* practitioner, the student was likely to want to intervene to prevent harm *(primum non nocere)*. Yet the expectation of a sociological observer (the professional stance to be adopted here by the medical student) is to minimize intervention. Thus, there is an initial role conflict between the expectations of the two professional roles that would be held simultaneously.

Complicating the case is the fact that a medical student is not yet a full-fledged professional but a professional in training. Thus, all the norms and maxims of the profession may not yet apply. Students are still expected to be learning and observing, not necessarily healing and helping. Does *primum non nocere* apply to this student? There is role ambiguity here as well as role conflict.

Faced with this dilemma, the Institutional Review Board that had to make the decision resolved the problem by calling for role clarity.[43] The board argued that third-year medical students have certain customary obligations that attach to their role as clinical clerks. They are members of a health care team, with some obligation to participate in the healing process. Patients expect medical students to have some knowledge and to act like doctors. Should the student step out of the healing role to become an investigator, the board felt that he should inform patients of the change in role and in its attendant expectations. This would protect patients from having unrealistic expectations, such as assuming that the medical student would tell them if he thought the course of treatment was harmful. The potential conflict between the student's role as helper and as observer was resolved by having the student spell out a list of specific conditions that

57

would have to be met before he would leave the observer role and intervene as a health care worker.

This resolution is based on the assumption that ethical obligations derive from our roles. If we can achieve clarity about the role or roles involved, and about our movement from one role to another, we will achieve more clarity about our ethical obligations as well. The existence of role ambiguity and conflict does not negate the importance of roles in determining ethical obligations.

Roles provide an initial link between the situation and appropriate norms for behavior. They also provide a mechanism for linking professional socialization and training with basic values and assumptions. Values and assumptions become embodied in our notions of what the role is and what it means to play it well. Should P administer medical aid when R is rushed into the emergency room? Much depends on what role P plays. Should Ruth break confidence? Much depends on how her role and its obligations are understood—by Ruth and by those with whom she interacts in the role (her "role-set"). Not all role expectations are explicit. Some are carried by images and models of the good professional. Both these implicit expectations and the explicit obligations of the role are important in determining what one ought to do in the situation.

This pivotal place of roles in morality can be diagrammed as follows:

Aims (of the profession)
Training (socialization)   Situation
Ideal Images, held by   } ⟶ ROLE(S)—— | —— Action
 —the profession   Norms
 —the society
 —the role-carrier

Roles are defined by the aims of the profession, the process of professional training and socialization, and the images of the good professional held by society, by the profession, and by the individual practitioner. Role definition in turn provides a link between norms and situations, suggesting what the role-holder should do when faced with a dilemma. To define or specify a role *is* in part to define a set of behaviors appropriate to the role and expected of those within it. The situation will call forth some of these behaviors.

Another important aspect of roles for looking at ethical dilemmas in professional practice is that roles endure. While a specific dilemma is a one-time phenomenon, the role and its expectations carry over from one situation to another. Roles are linked with images of whom to *be* as well as what to *do*. To talk about roles and their expectations points us in the direction of looking at who we *are* as professionals. This is the second important element in ethical decision making, and it is to this question that we turn in part II.

PART II
CHARACTER

4. BEING PROFESSIONAL

THE case of the medical student turning sociologist implies that once roles are clarified, ethical dilemmas are easily resolved—or at least they can then be structured to locate a solution. Confronting Ruth's ethical dilemma, therefore, it seems that if we could specify the aims, models, and images appropriate to ministers, such clarity about her role would resolve her ethical dilemma.

Yet denominational variation and changes in the definition of clergy role over time would appear to present a stumbling block to this effort. Even if the professional role is a morally relevant difference that should change Ruth's approach to her ethical dilemma, we may not be able to specify that role with sufficient clarity to assist her.

Being a Minister

But, denominational differences notwithstanding, there is overwhelming consensus on something central to the clergy role. From the earliest part of this century to the most recent, commentators are nearly unanimous in stressing one aspect of ministry. Nolan Harmon put it succinctly many years ago, "The Christian minister must *be* something before he can *do* anything. . . . His work depends on his personal character."[1]

That traditional note is sounded again and again through the decades: "What the minister *is* will be his greatest sermon";[2] "What he does is sometimes not nearly so important as what he is";[3] "I do not just *perform* a ministry,

I *am* a minister";[4] ". . . a ministry of being, not merely of doing."[5] Even as the face of ministry has changed, the theme of *being*, not merely *doing*, has remained.

Indeed, in the recent ATS "Readiness for Ministry" study, of the five leading characteristics affirmed for beginning ministers, four "center in the minister or priest as a person."[6] Similarly, the three images of ministers that were ranked least desirable among all denominations also dealt with issues of character.[7] All denominations were agreed that "service in humility" is most important.[8] While some might stress the "service" part of this phrase, I suggest that it is the inclusion of the phrase "in humility" that put this one at the top. It seems that character, not just function, is central to the professional role of clergy.

Some see this stress on character as growing clearly out of a theological base: it is because of the nature of the minister's calling that character looms so large. Thus William Hulme suggests that precisely because the minister is "a leader in faith" and because faith demands personal commitment, personal qualities become central.[9] Gustafson suggests, however, that the very lack of clear definition of clergy role is what has resulted in putting personality at a premium.[10] Southard proposes that the growth of American Protestantism was coupled with a clear rejection of certain forms of institutional authority. This had the effect of putting personal conversion at a premium—"pious character and fervent preaching" became the key to ministerial standing.[11]

Whether the roots of the stress on character are theological or sociological or both, for some commentators this stress is what distinguishes ministry from other professions. Owen Brandon argues that although ministry is a profession, the special standing of the minister has more to do with personal qualities than with professional role:

> The minister must learn to be a professional—to adopt the standards of the profession, to work like a professional, to achieve the expertise of the professional . . . —and then to

realize that he is accepted . . . not because of his "cloth," but because he is a sincere, humble, human person.[12]

Others argue that the charismatic nature of the minister's authority makes it questionable whether ministry can be classified as a profession at all. Urban Holmes argues that the professional model is not appropriate to ministry precisely because of its stress on character and person: "There seems to me to be a tendency in the professional model to emphasize skills that depend on a subject/object dichotomy; and the importance of the person or the professional is frequently lost."[13]

Whether ministry is appropriately considered a profession has been a controversial issue. Complicating the question is the fact that there is no single widely agreed upon definition of a profession. Yet most commentators agree upon a list of core characteristics shared by professions: (1) advanced training, including both (2) an intellectual component and (3) a specific body of skills to be applied (4) in the service of some (5) important societal function.[14] Some would add other characteristics: professional organization,[15] autonomy of practice,[16] or the dedication and discipline of the practitioner.[17] Of these, only "dedication" or the focus on "service" seems to touch on the concern for character that emerges as so central in ministry. It is no wonder, then, that some commentators take the view that the typical profession is characterized by a focus on knowledge, skill, organization, or other aspects of *task* and not by a concern for character or *being*.

Yet I think this is a mistaken view. To be sure, ministry will have its distinctive characteristics as a profession (some of these will be discussed in part III). But while a concern for character may receive special stress in ministry, it is not lacking in other professions. A look at professional codes provides a clue to the importance of this dimension of character for professional ethics generally, and begins to suggest some additional considerations important in making ethical decisions such as Ruth's.

Codes, Etiquette, and Morality

Professional codes of ethics specify role morality as it is understood by those within the profession. Codes are the place where special obligations or ways of balancing conflicting claims are enumerated. They tell professionals how to act *as a professional,* as understood by the professional group. Codes are considered one of the marks of a profession.[18] Their importance to the definition of professions may be seen in statements such as Dudley Strain's plea that the Christian minister "needs a code of ethics for his profession just as surely as every other professional . . . needs one."[19] While codes are debunked by outsiders, insiders are moving to adopt, amend, or strengthen their codes of professional ethics. Thus, if there are any special duties that emerge for professionals, they should emerge here. This is the first place we might look for what makes being a professional morally relevant in an ethical dilemma.

But professional codes have recently come under attack as having nothing at all to do with ethics! In a scathing critique, Lisa Newton dismisses them as "a code of Professional Manners oriented toward a Professional Image for the protection of Professional Compensation."[20] Noting that codes limit advertising, suppress competition, and forbid contradiction of professional judgments, Newton calls them a "gentlemanly etiquette designed to win that personal trust and popular confidence so very necessary for a respectable and appropriately lucrative career."[21]

Others have also charged that professional codes have more to do with money and etiquette than with ethics. June Goodfield rejects them as a clue to ethics: "Professional courtesy is not the same thing as professional morality, and medical ethics is by no means the same thing as medical etiquette, though these are usually confused or taken to be the same in the mind of the profession."[22] In his spoof on the importance of etiquette, Charles Smith suggests that young ministers study the "professional stance," for "the proper professional demeanor is much more important in acquiring and keeping clients than one's professional skill."[23] The "proper demeanor" includes "a black, oxford gray, or navy blue suit . . . of indifferent cut," a sedate sedan—"so as to obtain the optimum image reflection," and, above all, a pious air to suggest a certain detachment from worldly affairs.[24] While Smith does not suggest that these should be embodied in a code, there is a hint that professional codes are a second cousin to picayune etiquette.

The implications are clear: professional codes are not a guide to ethics, but simply protect professionals and ensure their status and income. They are the products of a guild that has as its first priority maintenance of itself.

Nor does this view lack supporting evidence. The principles of ethics of the American Dental Association (1972) include the explicit statement that they "are aimed primarily at upholding and strengthening dentistry as a full-fledged member of the learned professions."[25] A review of numerous professional codes reveals a tendency to reflect upon matters of deportment.[26] Codes often do sound like in-house documents designed to protect the elite status of the professionals involved.

Reinterpretation

My own view is that some of the disparagement of professional codes of ethics comes from viewing them in the wrong way and expecting them to do things that they cannot. When codes are approached as guidelines for specific behavior in specific circumstances, they rapidly demonstrate the twin problems of being too vague to be helpful or too rigid to adapt to the circumstances. Anyone who has tried to draft recommendations or regulations to govern behavior knows how extremely difficult it is to take a general ethical principle such as "respect for persons" and turn it into specific guidelines. Shall we say that in order to respect persons, informed consent is always necessary in the practice of medicine? Are there no circumstances in which we might actually endanger the person (and fail to be respectful) by waiting to get consent before we act? Can we possibly spell out all these in a code? If we state the requirement for consent categorically, we violate the meaning of the principle in some circumstances; yet if we simply say that one should be "respectful" of clients, we are too vague to be helpful.

I propose instead to understand professional codes a bit differently. Rather than looking for specific guidelines for *action* in professional codes, they might be better understood as statements about the *image* of the profession and the *character* of professionals.[27] Codes typically will indicate something of the kinds of ethical dilemmas that professionals encounter or expect to encounter, the loyalties they are expected to have, the tasks they perform, the locus of conflicts among role expectations, and so on. Understood this way, they become not codes for action, but guideposts to understand where stresses and tensions have been felt within the profession and what image of the good professional is held up to assist professionals through those stresses and tensions. This may provide an initial look at the "professional difference" when it comes to specific ethical dilemmas.

The Inside View: Embodying Norms

In their classic study of the professions,[28] Carr-Saunders and Wilson concluded that most professional codes are characterized by positive prescriptions on the one hand and negative sanctions (or grounds for expulsion from the profession) on the other. The reasons for exclusion or expulsion from membership range from illegal to improper behavior (e.g., sexual relations with clients).

The positive rules grew out of applications of the image of the priest and gentleman to contemporary problems. They include a service orientation, the necessity of upholding competence in practice (e.g., by not associating with those improperly trained or unqualified to practice), and the twin necessities of maintaining trust and confidentiality with clients while restricting the ways in which professionals can earn fees.

In this study, service, confidentiality, remuneration, and questions of competence emerged as crucial areas where ethical questions might arise and where the image of the profession would be at stake. While Carr-Saunders and Wilson noted that the rules incorporated into professional codes are quite diverse, they nonetheless argued that there is "a single ideal of conduct . . . based upon a few broad principles."[29]

More recently, C. S. Calian reviewed eight codes from diverse professions.[30] Like Carr-Saunders and Wilson, he found a "large measure of commonality" in the spirit and intent of their statements. Specifically, a majority of the codes incorporated statements on the following fifteen items:

1. A sense of calling or commitment;
2. The value of knowledge and skill; a requirement to provide "objective" diagnosis of problems;
3. A need to cooperate with colleagues;
4. A requirement of confidentiality toward the client;
5. The notion that service is primary, remuneration secondary;
6. The need for continuing education and improvement of skills;
7. The notion that the professional is sensitive to consumers' rights and well-being;
8. A requirement to be discrete in publications and not to solicit work openly;
9. A prohibition on misrepresenting one's credentials and the maintenance of strict standards for practice;
10. The derivation of one's primary income from the profession;
11. An affirmation of good citizenship;
12. A duty to recognize the limits of one's competence and call in consultants as needed;
13. A sense of the worth of the individual and of respect as the primary stance;
14. Requirements to reduce or eliminate conflicts of interest;
15. A requirement to keep oneself in good health.

A careful look at this list shows echoes of the concerns raised by Carr-Saunders and Wilson: service orientation is evident in items 1, 5, 7, and 14; stress on competence appears in items 2, 6, 9, 12, and possibly 3; the requirement for confidentiality is in item 4; and restrictions on remuneration appear in items 5, 8, and 10. While different codes will spell out these concerns in different ways, the underlying themes are indeed similar, and give support to the notion that there *is* a unifying view. Professional codes may provide a clue to professional ethics by suggesting the common themes that emerge around the concept of being a professional.

The unified view found by Carr-Saunders, Wilson, and Calian is a picture of the professional as (1) fair, (2) competent, (3) honest, (4) oriented toward the good of the client and of society, and (5) not taking advantage of clients (not abusing knowledge or power). This suggests that a number of ethical principles or prima facie duties lie behind ethical codes and find expression in them: justice, beneficence, non-maleficence, honesty, and fidelity.

Professional codes are not simply a matter of etiquette, then. Nor are they simply geared toward maintaining the "guild" or ensuring a "lucrative" career, as Newton and others charge. While they may have had the effect of serving these two functions, on a more fundamental level they present a picture of a professional person as one bound by certain ethical principles *and* as incorporating those principles *into his or her very character*. The professional is not merely expected not to tell a particular lie, but is expected to *be* an honest person.

In short, professional codes are geared primarily toward establishing expectations for character. Rather than looking to them for specific guidance on ethical dilemmas, it is more helpful to see them as incorporating an image of the *kind of person* the professional is supposed to be. Codes are geared toward patterns of behavior and the embodiment of general principles, not toward the spelling out of specific injunctions for behavior. Being honest requires such patterns of action as giving objective evaluations, not misrepresenting one's credentials, and so on. Being faithful includes not merely keeping confidence, but avoiding conflicts of interest, holding the well-being of the client as central, and so on. There is a relation between character and action, to be sure (we shall return to this in chapter 6). But the point here is that codes do not give specific guidance for action as much as they say something about the kinds of character traits necessary for someone to be a professional.

Professionalism

This may also help to explain why professionals tend to identify themselves and their personal lives with their professional service.[31] A professional is called not simply to *do* something but to *be* something. A professional "professes." Hence, although Charles Smith puts it facetiously, there is a grain of truth in his claim that "the public expects its professional[s] to act, talk, eat, drink, think, dress, and play in a manner which, in sum, reflects their profession."[32]

It is partly for this reason that Dorothy Emmet asserts that etiquette and ethics are not as far apart as some contemporary critics seem to assume.[33] Professional codes do reflect a concern for etiquette. This is not wrong, nor does it prevent them from being meaningful statements of ethics as well. However, the ethics to which they point is primarily an ethics of character, not of action. Codes may be couched in actional language ("do this," "avoid that"), but their meaning emerges only when we look behind these specifics to a sense of the overall picture of the type of person who is to *embody* those actions. Etiquette is related, because it has to do with elements of style that indicate whether a person will be successful at embodying a certain type of character.

Given this fact, it is tempting to look for what is morally relevant about being in a professional role in some concept of *professionalism* rather than in role expectations per se. Many commentators on professional life stress the sense of responsibility felt by professionals for their work. Carr-Saunders and Wilson discuss "professionalism" and "the professions" without any clear demarcation between these concepts.[34] Central to being a professional is a sense of professionalism. What we expect of professionals is not simply a *task* to be done, but a *way* of doing it. Questions of style and attitude may be central to professional ethics.

Public images reinforce this idea. When we charge someone with unprofessional behavior, we often have in mind not simply the act itself, but the *way* in which it is done. Certain types of behavior come to be expected of people in a role, and failure to act in accord with those expectations opens one to the charge of unprofessional behavior. To enter a professional role is not simply to take on certain duties, but to take on an entire complex of expectations about behavior, including both function and style. A minister who fails to keep confidence will not simply be thought to be a bit of a gossip, but will be accused of unprofessional behavior.

Similarly, negative images associated with the term *professional* are largely questions of style and attitude. Professionals are often seen as "cold," "distant," "analytical," "stuck up," and the like.[35] Interestingly, these very qualities may come to be associated with proper professionalism, so that a minister who is warm and emotional rather than cold and analytical will be seen as unprofessional. All of this suggests that the professional difference, if any, may lie in some concept of the *style* with which the work is done, not in distinctions as to the type of work performed. It may not be that there are special duties for professionals, then, but simply that professionals are expected to do their duties with a particular demeanor.

This focus on style rather than task seems to be further reinforced by the growing tendency to use the term *professional* to apply to all sorts of work that formerly would not have been associated with professions. My local newspaper advertises professional window cleaning, professional plant care, professional plumbing, and even professional cat-sitting! If it is accurate to use the term *professional* to apply to these occupations, then surely it is the *style* in which the work is done or the *thoroughness* with which it is done that renders it professional. And if style is all that counts, then surely the term *professional* becomes a bit meaningless, as some critics have charged.[36]

Integrity

And yet, style is not all there is to the sense of professionalism embodied in codes. Two professionals can play the same role in quite different styles. A nice bedside manner does not necessarily mean that we are in the hands of a good doctor. Though we may be more comfortable with one style rather than the other—and may indeed choose our professionals on the basis of style—the other practitioner is still a professional. Style is something the individual brings to the role, but it is not the same as the role.[37]

Indeed, we would not even use the term *professional* to designate style were it not for the history of the professions and the kinds of expectations that have come to be associated with them. It is the history behind the professions and the expectations of those in them that now permit us to use the term *professional* to speak of any job when it is well done. What the term seems to suggest is that those in professional roles are expected not only to do their jobs, but to do them with a certain level of *integrity*.

In short, at the core of code morality is the notion of professional character. It is not simply that the work is done well, but that the person brings a certain kind of integrity to it. As Emmet suggests, the behavior embodied in codes may originally have been put there for functional reasons: if one keeps confidence, clients will be more likely to divulge information that is necessary for the professional to determine how to help them. However, over time the behavior comes to be valued in itself and is taken as a mark of integrity.[38] There *is* a style or demeanor associated with being a professional, but it is not *simply* a matter of style and demeanor. It is also a matter of character and integrity.

Central to professional integrity as seen in codes are both *competence* and *commitment*. Edmund Pellegrino argues that "competence has become the first ethical precept for the modern physician, after integrity."[39] Similarly, Bayles argues that competence is "perhaps the most crucial characteristic" in professional ethics, derived from a basic notion of trustworthiness or integrity.[40]

When we turn from other professions to ministry, we find that "while the expectation of ministry or priesthood in North America includes competence in functions, it is also highly sensitive to the character and spirit of the person."[41] Thus, both competence and commitment are held up, but the order of their importance may be reversed.[42] This may be partly because of the standards used to assess ministerial competence: "The competence of the minister is measured by his ability to incarnate godly concern for others and convey this realistically."[43] It is also because of the general stress on total identification of the clergy with their work: "Gradually his work becomes his life and his life becomes his work."[44]

What all of this suggests is that professions share a concern for "being" as well as "doing." To be sure, the focus on "being" in ministry seems to be stronger. Yet an analysis of professional codes suggests that other professions also care about the integrity and character of their practitioners.[45] They expect not simply well-trained people who know what to do and are competent at performing their functions, but people of commitment and dedication who *care* about their clients. This is perhaps why codes tend to include statements stressing respect for the client, humility about one's skills, and so on. (Some codes go so far as to require that professionals avoid "even the appearance" of impropriety.)[46] These are rudimentary statements about virtue; they have to do with dispositions and attitudes that change our moral evaluation of acts. We shall return to this question in chapter 5.

Toward an Ethics of Character

In sum, we have seen that professional codes are not at all devoid of ethics. Their injunctions may seem strange at first glance, but they can be seen to derive from and point to a number of prima facie duties—justice, promise keeping, truth telling, beneficence, and non-maleficence. As we saw above, prima facie duties are not distinctive to professionals. But professional codes suggest how these universal principles are worked out for particular groups. In this sense, they develop the role-morality of which Dorothy Emmet speaks; they are concerned with "how one should act in a certain capacity."[47]

At the same time, we have seen that they are more meaningful when interpreted as an ethics of character or virtue than simply as an ethics of action. They tell the professional not only what to *do* but whom to *be.* It is not simply that one is to distribute goods fairly; this would be justice in action. But the codes require something broader: the professional is to be fair in *all* her dealings. Similarly, it is not merely that one is to tell the truth about one's qualifications; the professional is expected to be a truthful *person.*

It is the sense of integrity that underlies the codes and that is central, then, to being a professional as seen from the "inside." Professionals are expected to exhibit a high level of responsibility—toward the client, toward the quality of work, toward the profession and other colleagues, and (at least to some extent) toward society. As Carr-Saunders and Wilson suggest, there is indeed a "single ideal of conduct . . . based upon a few broad principles." But the ideal of conduct is not simply a set of rules to follow or actions to avoid or encourage. It is a sense of doing what one does in the right way, with the right attitude—with integrity. The ideal of conduct is an ideal for the *person,* not just for the person's actions. We have begun to move, then, toward an ethics of character.

This helps to explain why ministers confronted with Ruth's dilemma about keeping confidence often answered in terms of their sense of integrity: "I just couldn't do that; it would violate my sense of who I am." Some who felt that breaking confidence could be *justified* by rational argument—and who could not find arguments as compelling for keeping confidence—nonetheless "knew" that they had to keep confidence. Some answered in terms of their sense of Ruth's development as a professional: "Well, her whole career is at stake here; but I guess if you can't take the risks early on, you won't ever amount to much in the profession."

These statements are consonant with those professional codes that express the inside view of what it means to be a good professional—a person of integrity who not only does the "right" thing, but is an *honorable person.* There *is* a difference between doing the right thing and being an honorable person. Though it is difficult to specify this difference, intuition tells us that we want not simply to do what is right, but to *be* a good person—or minister, or professional. It is to these questions of character and virtue, and the link between being and doing, that we turn in the next two chapters.

5. THE
TRUSTWORTHY
TRUSTEE

IN professional codes, professionals are encouraged not simply to *do* or avoid doing certain things, but to *be* or become a certain kind of person. When dealing with professional roles such as ministry, the images and ideals that attend the role have a lot to do with character and integrity. In particular, professionals such as Ruth must be both competent and committed. From a concern about what Ruth should *do* when confronted with a concrete and difficult ethical dilemma regarding confidentiality, we have moved to a concern for who she should *be*.

This is not strange. In everyday life, we often respond to ethical dilemmas by urging virtues or stances toward the world rather than action. We exhort people to "be brave," "be fair," "be patient," not just "do this," "avoid that." It is normal to think about ethical issues not only in terms of right behavior, but also in terms of appropriate feelings, attitudinal responses, and ways of being. We urge the person to *be* a certain way, not just to *do* something. This raises questions of virtue and character.

We have already seen (chapter 1) that rules often conflict, particularly in difficult cases. Indeed, what makes an ethical dilemma a *dilemma* is precisely that there is no single rule that can easily be applied. Thus, though we may generally seek to resolve dilemmas by looking for a rule that can apply to the case, in most instances we find that there is more than one rule—or more than one prima facie duty—that applies. In Ruth's case, for example, there are several rules that apply:

"keep promises," "do good," and "treat people with respect." If Ruth is genuinely convinced that she cannot do good or respect the rights of others unless she breaks a promise, the two-step process that looks for a rule to apply simply is not useful. What, then, is she to do?

In a number of instances, looking for a rule to apply is not very helpful. For example, the rules may be uncertain, or we may not have sufficient clarity about how our situation fits under them. The rules themselves may make us uncomfortable or the action to which they point may seem inconsistent with our moral code in general. Or the situation may be unprecedented in our moral career. Professional life is full of such "firsts" where we seem not to have an obvious answer or a rule immediately available to resolve the dilemma. In any of these cases, a simple rule-oriented approach to deciding what to do does not suffice.[1]

Both Mayo and Frankena suggest that at this point, *virtue* becomes central. As Frankena puts it, "I need not ask, 'What ought I to do? . . .' I can also, quite naturally, ask, 'What is the good or virtuous thing to do?' "[2] That is, we could start with an ethics of virtue, with "aretaic" judgments about good and bad character. When we ask what to do, then, the answer would take the form of a command to *be* something: be patient, be brave, and so on. We can supplement our usual concern for right action by a concern for good character. Indeed, the concern for good character is not only a "supplement" but may be integral to solving the dilemma, for, as Stanley Hauerwas suggests, "The kind of decisions we confront, indeed the very way we describe a situation, is a function of the kind of character we have."[3]

A perspective that focuses on questions of character, virtue, and "being," rather than on rules, situations, and right action alone, brings at least two additional dimensions to ethical analysis.

The Depth and Breadth of Our Acts

First it helps to account for the depth and breadth of our acts. As suggested above, there is a kind of unity to urging

Ruth to "be fair" or "be honest" or "be trustworthy" that goes beyond specific rules and decisions about keeping confidence. To say "be trustworthy" is to urge more than simply keeping confidence. Trustworthiness is a multifaceted quality of persons. The trustworthy person does not simply keep confidence, but is thoughtful about the impact of her decisions on others, sensitive to their needs and claims, and so on. Similarly, an honest person is not merely one who tells no lies. We can sometimes avoid lying by simply withholding information; but the other person remains deceived. When we describe a person as honest, we generally have in mind someone who tries to avoid any kind of deception, not just explicit lies.

It is for this reason that Bayles proposes that the standards for a "good" or trustworthy professional include not simply honesty and confidentiality, but "candor" and "discretion."[4] Candor goes a bit beyond the strict requirements of honesty—it requires not only truthfulness in what is disclosed, but full disclosure. Similarly, discretion is broader than confidentiality—it requires not simply holding secret what has been shared, but holding secret additional knowledge gained about the client from other sources.

There is a breadth implied in professional judgment that is not always well suited by strict rules of keeping confidence or telling the truth. The language of virtue, or "being," may be better suited to describe that breadth. That is why I suggested in chapter 4 that the professional tries to emulate an ideal of the honorable person. To be honorable is not simply to do the "right" thing. It is to "be good" as well as to "do right." As Mayo suggests, heroes and saints "are not merely people who did things. They are people whom we are expected, and expect ourselves, to imitate."[5] But imitating does not just mean doing what they did. It means trying to *be* like them. The ideals that are captured in the stories of heroes and saints go beyond principles into images of the kinds of people we want to be.

Second, there is not only the question of the breadth of decisions to be made, but of their depth—the continuity over time between this decision and others. Ruth, for example, must consider the impact of any decision she makes on the kinds of quandaries that will face her in the future. If she keeps confidence, and Kathy continues in her quest for an abortion, is Ruth now obligated in any way to assist her? Should she offer to accompany Kathy? Should she help to pay for the services? It is difficult to answer these questions in the language of "doing" alone. Why would keeping confidence obligate Ruth to do anything further? What does keeping confidence have to do with accompanying Kathy as she implements her decision? If we look at this case in terms of quandaries about discrete actions, each of which requires a separate moral decision, they seem disconnected and there is no easy way to argue from one to the other.

Yet in conversation with ministers about this case, one of the first issues that comes up is always: "If I don't tell anyone else, then I would be implicated and I must go with her and help her. I might even have to lend her the money." Why are these assumptions made about the need to follow through and provide additional care?

We might try to explain this sense of ongoing responsibility in terms of the effects of our actions. If I promise to do something, part of the meaning of making that promise is that I will subsequently do what I said. Hence, what I say today may obligate me to act in the future. This is sometimes called the "performative" role or aspect of language.[6] Language does not simply describe or respond to situations, but can itself create situations. It sets up expectations on the part of others. As Paul Ramsey puts it, "The words, 'I promise' . . . are performative in the sense that they create and establish the relationship or moral bond to which they refer and that did not exist before."[7] When I say that I promise something, what I say is not simply a statement but is a way of changing the world. Thus, Ruth's promise today can implicate her tomorrow.

However, the performative nature of language does not alone give a totally satisfactory explanation for the continuity of action. If Ruth promises to keep confidence, the performative effect of this utterance lies in the expectation that she will then indeed keep confidence. The only future obligation that she has established is not to say anything further. There is no easy connection between her obligation to keep silent about what she knows and any other obligations for action. Why should she feel obligated not only to keep silent but to provide help, to offer financial assistance, or to go with Kathy? And why should she feel *more* obligated to provide help once she decides to keep confidence? The link between two discrete actions or decisions is difficult to establish if we think only in terms of rules for behavior.

We may be better able to explain our sense of broader obligations if we turn from the language of duty to the language of character. Character gives continuity from one action to another. While actions may be discrete, the person or moral *agent* who acts is the same person. Her or his different actions over time must somehow fit into a whole that makes sense.[8]

Suppose, for example, that in view of Kathy's seeming lack of community, Ruth judges it important to be her friend.[9] Hence, she decides to keep confidence.

Note, first, the way in which she has posed the issue: I want to be a friend; therefore I must keep confidence. As noted above, when we are trying to decide what to do, we often do so in terms of whom we want to *be,* and what actions we think will display those qualities. The decision about whom to *be* precedes the decision about what to *do.*

Note also that this desire to *be* a friend is what then puts Ruth under additional obligation to Kathy. How does a friend act? Perhaps the first act is not to break confidence. But there are others implied as well. The friend does not abandon the other—hence, Ruth must go with Kathy through the abortion process if necessary, and possibly must also assist in finding financial resources. And, of course, there are other things that a friend might do as well—making sure that Kathy has all the information necessary to make a good decision, providing perspectives that Kathy may not see, and probing to the deepest levels of the meaning of Kathy's contemplated act.

A simple decision about whether it is wrong to break confidence might not have led to these further issues. It is the link between what we are to *do* and whom we wish to *be* that helps to explain why certain kinds of questions arise as we think about an ethical dilemma. To be a friend or to be trustworthy implies a whole host of actions and issues that might otherwise not be perceived in a dilemma about keeping confidence. If we look behind the seeming rules for action that are provided in professional codes ("keep confidence") and ask what kinds of character those rules support (being trustworthy), it becomes clear why we cannot simply settle for doing what the rule ostensibly requires. To be trustworthy requires a kind of continuity both in breadth of actions and in depth that goes beyond individual acts of keeping confidence. It may require an entire set of additional actions.

Indeed, it is possible that posing the issue in terms of whom we wish to *be*—for example, "being trustworthy"—might require the breaking of confidence! At first, this seems a shocking proposal, since breaking confidence would obviously seem like a violation of trust to Kathy. How, then, could it be required by a concern to be trustworthy?

Consider the following possibility. Several ministers responding to this case quickly pointed out that Kathy may be manipulating Ruth, whether consciously or not. She corners Ruth, sets the stage, calls the shots by defining the situation, and puts Ruth on the spot.[10]

What does it mean for a minister to be trustworthy in a situation in which she is being manipulated? Simply responding to the overt request—e.g., the request for financial assistance—may not be the most trustworthy response. If Kathy is manipulating Ruth, she may also be manipulating others; indeed, the pregnancy may be a conscious or unconscious means of doing so. Thus, the conversation needs to address these issues if the professional is to be trustworthy on the deepest level.[11] In some cases, it might not be possible to do so without breaking confidence.

To be trustworthy, therefore, cannot be captured easily by any single rule or set of rules, such as "keep confidence." Part of being trustworthy means being able to deal with issues on their deepest level—this is what makes the professional worthy of trust, and it is why professional training and competence are so often stressed. Professional codes that require competence and include rules about keeping confidence are best understood as pointing to the virtue of trustworthiness.

The language of character and virtue provides a kind of continuity that the language of duty, decision, and right action does not seem able to offer. It helps to explain why we think of ethical dilemmas in terms of sets of action or patterns of action, and not just in terms of doing a single right act. It accounts for the "spreading" effect of our decisions and for the continuity of character that accompanies decisions. It explains why our integrity can sometimes seem to be at stake in a single act.[12]

Character and Story

If accounting for the breadth and depth of action is the first advantage gained by using the language of virtue or character, the second is equally important. The language of being accounts for something that is altogether missing from the language of doing: the impact of our actions on ourselves. As James McClendon suggests, a focus solely on decision making or ethical quandaries tends to restrict morality into a kind of case law. It ignores the moral qualities of the people involved.[13] Yet equally important with the act itself is the moral agent who performs it.

Indeed, when we act, we not only *do* something, we also shape our own character. Our choices about what to do are also choices about whom to be. A single lie does not necessarily make us a liar; but a series of lies may. And so each choice about what to *do* is also a choice about whom to *be*—or, more accurately, whom to become.[14]

We see this also in everyday life. Suppose a young couple have always wanted children and have an image of themselves as "good parents." They see themselves as loving and faithful people who want to be co-creators with God and who believe that they have the patience to raise children and do it well. Now this same couple are told that they are at risk for a genetic disorder in their children. They are offered prenatal diagnosis with the possibility of selective abortion.

How do they reconcile abortion—the destruction of their own child—with their image of themselves as loving, caring, and faithful parents? How do they reconcile the rejection of a child because of a genetic disorder with their description of themselves as patient and responsible parents? The act of abortion seems directly contrary to their image of themselves as loving parents. How could I do such a thing? they ask. The question means: How could a person like me—or like the person I want to be—do such a thing *without becoming a different person*?[15]

A contemplated act can contradict the image we have of ourselves. If part of our role expectations comes out of images we have of the "ideal" role-holder, then sometimes an act will be so contrary to that ideal that it seems we cannot both do the act and continue to think of ourselves as a good person in the role. Can a minister break confidence and still be a faithful person or a good minister? Will Ruth become a different person if she does something that seems to contradict her image of herself—and the expectations that she and others have of a minister? If Ruth wants to model trustworthiness for her church—to embody her understanding of God's covenant with humankind—then would she be able to break confidence? It is in this sense that even a seemingly small act can threaten a person's integrity.

Not all acts change our character or threaten our integrity, of course. Some acts fit our image and reinforce the person we are in process of becoming. If we choose to do them, we are also choosing to accept—and even strengthen—the person we already are. But other acts cannot easily be reconciled with the image we have of ourselves. There may be no way to do the act without changing our self-description. We *become* different people. We must either choose not to do the act, or we must accept the new image of ourselves that accompanies it. (And, of course, the temptation to deceive ourselves about what we have done may be very great: I am not untrustworthy; I did it out of love.)[16]

In short, as we act we create ourselves. Each of us has a story, a biography. That story links the disparate elements of our lives into a coherent whole. We all know how crucial a random childhood event can be. Sometimes we spend the rest of our lives living out the meaning of a single event, or trying to wipe something from our memory.[17] The things that happen to us, and the things that we do in response to the world around us, make us who we are. Our actions can reinforce our character, or they can change our character.

What gives a person integrity is the way the events of his or her life fit together into a pattern that makes sense. When we think of people as having integrity or having character, we think of them as living their lives in such a way that they are predictable to some extent. We can guess how they will respond to the next crisis because we have seen how they responded before. While consistency alone does not make for integrity, the events of people's lives and the actions they choose must at least have coherence in order for their life stories to make sense and to exhibit character or integrity. To have integrity means that reasons can be given for seemingly aberrant behavior; the whole of the person's actions and life coheres.[18]

Thus, another possible test for any contemplated action is to ask whether it fits our life story. Does it lend integrity to us, or does it threaten our integrity? Many ministers responded to Ruth's case by asking, "Could I do this with integrity?" Some said, "I don't like to interfere with my parishioners' decisions, but abortion is pretty serious stuff; it doesn't seem consistent with the 'good news' that I try to live." Others said, "If I violate confidence, I've really stopped being a minister." Just as we saw in chapter 3 that professionals often model their actions on some ideal image or role model, so they also can ask whether an action contributes to making them into the kind of person they wish to be. Does it help them *become* the person they want to emulate? When confronted with a difficult ethical dilemma, we can ask not merely, Is this the right thing to do? but, Which act has the most integrity in terms of the kind of person I want to become?

Virtue and Role

To some extent, this is a private question. For example, Ruth has her own private image of the person she wants to be. She may be modeling her life after the biblical story of Ruth, her namesake. If so, then she will undoubtedly seek those qualities of character—faithfulness, willingness to risk, endurance through hardship, and courage to be a "stranger in a strange land"—that characterize the biblical story.

However, some virtues or character traits may also be role-related or even role-specific. Each profession might have its particular virtues. Maurice Mandelbaum proposes that nursing may require a kind of "buoyancy" that we would not expect in other professions.[19] Our stereotypes of professionals often suggest these virtues: tenacity for lawyers, gentleness for pediatricians, cheerfulness for nurses, piety for ministers, and so on. (Note that pushed to extremes, these virtues can become vices—tenacity becomes pigheadedness, cheerfulness becomes an inability to accept tragedy, and so on.)

There may also be some virtues that apply to professionals in general. If all professional groups share some characteristics, and if there are general role expectations (of competence, honesty, beneficence, etc.) that apply to the professions in general, then there are likely to be some virtues for professionals in general. These would apply to clergy, though of course there might be additional role-specific virtues as well.[20]

Trustworthiness

And indeed, this is what I believe we find. Just as we noted that professional codes of ethics can be best understood as statements about character, and that they point to a particular understanding of integrity, so the image of professionals that is lifted up in codes and in the traditional view of the professions held by society suggests that there is a virtue central for the character of any professional.

The great American sociologist Talcott Parsons has provided us with a term for the professions that helps to indicate this primary virtue. In reviewing the meaning and the history of the professions, Parsons concludes that professionals are distinguished by the "independent trusteeship . . . of a major part of the cultural tradition of the society."[21] Other sociologists following Parsons have stressed the independence or autonomy of professionals.[22] But I think if we focus instead on the notion of *trustee,* we will have a clue to the virtues of professionals.

We sometimes think of the term with reference to being the trustee for someone's estate. It can imply taking over and making decisions on behalf of another. Public outcry against professions has focused precisely on these aspects of taking over and being paternalistic. I shall return to this issue in part III. Here, I am concerned not with whether power is abused but with why power is given in the first place. What are the qualities that would inspire us to make someone a trustee?

The term *trustee* implies that power is given over something that is of *value.*[23] In the case of professionals, Parsons locates this value in some major part of the cultural tradition. For example, physicians are entrusted with knowledge and power in the area of physical health, lawyers in the area of social and interpersonal relations. Ministers are entrusted with the part of the cultural tradition that has to do with our relations to God or to the spiritual realm—the soul.[24] In each case, the profession is entrusted by society with power in an area that is crucial to the well-being of people. For this reason, Bernard Barber calls the knowledge of professionals a "powerful" knowledge.[25]

The one who is to be entrusted with something valuable or crucial to human well-being must be trustworthy—worthy of what is entrusted. Knowledge and power (or control over a cultural tradition) are given over in order that the trustees may serve society, not, for example, to aggrandize themselves. In short, reciprocity is implied: something of value is given so that something else of value may be gained. The freedom granted to professionals in their work and in developing their fields of knowledge is granted in the conviction that this is the best way to foster the service desired.[26]

It is also granted in the conviction (or assumption, which is now being challenged) that those to whom it is given are *trustworthy*.[27] The exchange implies a crucial role for promise keeping, confidentiality, and honesty in the relations between professionals and their clients and between the professions and society. It implies that professionals must be worthy of trust.

When we listed the qualities of professionals that are embodied in professional codes, a few emerged as central: the professional is honest, fair, helpful, not hurtful, and so on. The term *trustworthy* did not appear on this list. However, it might be taken to be the underlying theme that links these other qualities together. One who is honest, fair, helpful, and not hurtful can be *trusted*—trusted to work for the good of the client, not for her own good; trusted to tell the truth and know the limits of his expertise; and so on. All of these qualities taken together imply a person who is trustworthy.

To have integrity as a professional is largely to have those qualities that render one trustworthy. The professional is the trustworthy trustee. The stress on honesty, beneficence, non-maleficence, and the like in professional codes is not intended to be a list of rules for behavior so much as *an assurance of trustworthiness* to the public, and an indication to the professional of the central virtue of professional status.[28] It tells both the public and the practicing professional that this person, in order to be in this profession, must be trustworthy. The implication is that anyone found not to be trustworthy will be ousted.

This helps to explain in part why we react more strongly when scientists lie or falsify data than we do when politicians lie.[29] It is not that we condone lying per se. Lying remains wrong. But truth is at the heart of scientific research in a way that it is not at the heart of politics. Thus, when a scientist lies, it undermines not only our sense of the trustworthiness of the person but of the profession, and possibly of the entire social order. "If you can't trust a doctor, whom can you trust?"

If we take an "aretaic" or virtue-centered approach to ethical dilemmas and ask not, What should I do? but, Who should I be? the first answer for professionals emerges as, be trustworthy. While this does not give much concrete guidance, it does suggest some directions that are possible and some that are less plausible. For example, if Ruth broke confidence, she would surely be seen by Kathy as not trustworthy. Trying to be trustworthy will tend to push Ruth in the direction of keeping confidence. Focusing on the virtue of trustworthiness helps to explain why the requirement of confidentiality appears in almost every professional code, and why the violation of this requirement looms so large and seems so devastating to professionals and clients alike.

Judas

Like other professionals, ministers are expected to be trustworthy. However, the expectation is heightened in their case: they are not only to be trustworthy but to be *exemplary* in their trustworthiness.[30] "Misconduct is inexcusable in any profession, but it is glaringly so among preachers."[31] Any small breach of trust becomes a large breach. Some have taken this to mean that the minister is expected to be superhuman and is not permitted normal human faults and foibles.[32] I take it a bit differently. The minister is expected to embody trustworthiness in such an integral way (i.e., to have such integrity) that even the slightest failure becomes a sign of lack of integrity. This does not mean that the minister is permitted no faults. It means that the minister is permitted no faults *that have to do with trustworthiness*.

This is no doubt in part because ministers are understood to be entrusted not only by society, but also by God. Many ministers would protest the idea that they are given their profession by society. As Brita Gill argues, "Ultimately our authority as women or men in ministry has its source in our vocation as servants of Jesus Christ. It is God who grants us authority."[33] This vocation from God is also perceived by parishioners. But what it means for them largely is that the minister is expected to be Christ-like, living a life that demonstrates God's love for humankind. And in what does that love consist?—in faithful covenant, the Hebrew *hesed,* or steadfast love.[34] Hence, if the minister is supposed to symbolize God's covenanting and redeeming activity toward humankind, this will mean an even greater stress on being trustworthy.

This becomes evident if we look at the central Christian story. Jesus might well have been found by the authorities and put to death without having been betrayed by Judas. Why, then, do we have Judas in the story? If Jesus' death and resurrection are central to the Christian story, why not omit Judas' act from the recounting of it? Why is Judas so important in this story?

The importance of Judas resides in lifting up to us the sense of betrayal. What Judas does in that story is to show the importance of violation of trust, and God's actions in the face of that violation. Judas' betrayal provides the contrast to God's faithfulness. The inclusion of Judas in the story tells us that the one in whom we can trust would *not* betray us—would neither reveal our location to the authorities nor bring harm to us.

The role of Judas in the story of Jesus' death and resurrection thus demonstrates the centrality of trustworthiness for those who follow Christ. It also suggests the importance of retaining theological language. When someone in whom we have trusted proves to be not trustworthy— violates a confidence, deceives us, lies about us to others—we feel *betrayed.* This term captures the meaning of violation of trust better than any other I know. Adrienne Rich's powerful portrait of the experience of loss of trust—the bleak, jutting ledge that brings us close to formlessness[35]—is best captured by the term *betrayal.*

The minister who violates trust is not simply unprofessional, therefore. This person has not only failed to exhibit the central virtue of the professional, but is seen as being like Judas and hence violating the command to follow Jesus. If breaking confidence means that we cease to be trustworthy, then we have not simply *done* the wrong thing. We have *been* the wrong person—Judas instead of Jesus. In terms of the stories that give shape to the lives of professionals, the untrustworthy minister becomes the betrayer like Judas. This helps to explain why there is special emphasis on trustworthiness for ministers. It does not negate the importance of trustworthiness for all professionals, however.

I shall argue in part III that being trustworthy is not enough for professionals. Indeed, the traditional emphasis on the trustworthiness of professionals may be part of the reason for the collapse of confidence in the professions today. However, limited though trustworthiness alone is as a basis for professional ethics, it goes far toward explaining the basic virtue that is expected of professionals both by the profession itself and by others. Many professionals, encountering difficult ethical dilemmas, ask not simply, What should I do? but, How can I be trustworthy here? The decision about what to *do* is in part a reflection of whom they wish to *be*.

6. FROM VIRTUE TO VISION: THE PRUDENT PROFESSIONAL

WE saw in chapter 5 that the language of "doing" does not account for all our felt obligations. Sometimes we feel an obligation to go beyond what would strictly seem to be required in the situation. We also assume that our actions today set up ongoing obligations for tomorrow. The language of "virtue" or "character" seems to account better than the language of duty for both these phenomena.

We also saw that the history of the professions suggests that a primary virtue for professionals is *trustworthiness*. This virtue reflects the internal expectations of professional groups as expressed in professional codes. It also explains some expectations placed on professionals by their clients, evidenced in the sense of betrayal and shock when a professional—particularly a minister—fails to be trustworthy.

But how does this help us when we are trying to make a difficult ethical decision? Telling Ruth to be trustworthy or to develop certain virtues hardly seems to resolve her question about whether to break confidence. To tell Ruth to be trustworthy is not enough; we need to know what kind of action will be implied by this command as well as what kind of character is to be developed.

Being and Doing

What is the relationship between being a good or virtuous person and doing the right thing? Virtues and vices are traits of character. They have to do with the *motivations* from which we act.[1] To do something from good motives (such as a desire to help) does not necessarily mean that we will do the right thing.

For instance, suppose Ruth decides to break confidence. However, suppose she does so not out of genuine desire to help Kathy but out of fear that her job will be in jeopardy if the confidence is discovered. We might think that Ruth made the right choice in divulging the information but question her motives or even find them reprehensible. Conversely, we might think that someone does the wrong thing, but for the right reasons. If Ruth breaks confidence out of a desire to help Kathy, we might think it was the wrong thing to do, but still find her motives commendable.

Thus, it is possible to say that someone did the right thing but was not virtuous, and it is also possible to say that someone exhibited virtue but did the wrong thing. The link between virtue and action, being and doing, is not a simple one-to-one correlation in which a right act always indicates a virtuous person and a wrong act always indicates a nonvirtuous person.[2] A wrong act is not necessarily a vicious act, nor does it point to a vicious agent. A right act is not necessarily done by a virtuous person.

And yet there is *some* link between action and virtue. How would we form our judgments of who is good and bad except by looking at the person's actions? As Mayo puts it, you can't just *be;* you can only be by *doing.*[3] We know who we are only by assessing what we do. While a single lie does not make a person dishonest, a pattern of lies does. Patterns of action over time form the basis for our judgments about a person's character and virtues. If Ruth breaks confidence once, we might nonetheless think her a trustworthy person. But if breaking confidence becomes a habit for her, at some point we would judge her untrustworthy. In this way, being and doing are related. There may not be a direct, one-to-one correlation between them, but there is at least an indirect link.

Thus, asking about virtue should give us some clue to right action. And yet the link seems very indirect. I suggested in part I that actions are right or wrong depending on how they reflect the appropriate prima facie duties in the situation. The *motives* out of which the act is done would seem to be irrelevant to the rightness of the act. How, then, could we derive a decision about what to do from an examination of virtues, which have primarily to do with motivation? Or, to put it another way, no matter how important people think character is for a professional, good character does not ensure that Ruth will do the right thing.

Yet the link between virtue and action may be closer than first appears. Mandelbaum distinguishes two types of virtue: "actional" and "dispositional" virtues. Careful attention to the distinction may help us to see a clearer link between virtue and deciding what to do.

According to Mandelbaum, actional virtues are traits of character that emerge in response to the concrete demands of a situation and that seem fitting as a response to that situation. When a child wanders into the street in front of an oncoming truck, a woman who rushes into the street to rescue the child exhibits courage. She need not have acted out of a particular feeling (love); indeed, she may not have had time to think at all about what she was doing. She simply reacted to the situation, and demonstrated bravery in that action.

But note that it is not the *behavior* alone that makes the act virtuous. Rushing into the street in front of oncoming vehicles could be a sign of foolhardiness. But *in this situation* in which a child's life is in danger, the circumstances seem to call for such an action. Hence, as Mandelbaum puts it, "The essence of an actional virtue lies in the fact that such a trait is seen as a means of meeting an objective demand which the situation is held to place upon the agent."[4] This first kind of virtue, then, has to do with acting in accord with the objective demands of a situation.

Dispositional virtues are different from actional virtues. They may not take the form of concrete actions at all, but of a stance toward the world or a tendency to see the world in certain ways. Gratitude is a dispositional virtue. It is exhibited in the tendency to see oneself as the recipient of unearned gifts, to be thankful toward others, and so on. Unlike courage, which can be demonstrated either in a single act or in a pattern of action over time (e.g., a refusal to yield under torture), the dispositional virtue of gratitude is not likely to be attributed to someone on the basis of a *single* thank-you. It is, rather, the person's overall stance and manner that seem to give rise to this designation. The dispositional virtue is precisely what its name suggests—a disposition, a way of seeing and perhaps of feeling about the world.

Mandelbaum suggests that actional traits have to do with *responding* to the concrete demands of the situation, while dispositional virtues have to do with *perceiving* those demands. There can be, then, two kinds of vice: first, a failure to be sensitive to the demands of the situation, and second, a failure to be motivated by those demands even when they are perceived—e.g., callousness and cruelty.

The importance of this analysis for our purposes is this: it shows that virtues are not totally separate from the objective demands of the situation, or from the "right" thing to do. Some virtues have to do with responding appropriately to the demands of the situation. Others have to do with perceiving those demands adequately and being motivated by them. Similarly, Arthur Dyck argues for two virtues which he calls "moral perceptivity" and "moral tenacity." These are the virtues of discerning moral claims and having a disposition toward the good, respectively.[5]

Drawing on Dyck and Mandelbaum, we see that those traits of character called virtues are not totally separable from our judgments about what the situation demands. We make a judgment that someone is courageous only in a situation in which courage is called for. We judge someone grateful only because of his or her sensitivity to certain aspects of situations. Thus, virtues have at least an indirect relation to right action: they dispose us to perceive what is required and to do it.

It seems, then, that virtues provide another link between the situation and what we are to do. They are the terms we use to describe certain kinds of response to situational demands, or certain tendencies to be sensitive to what those demands might be. Just as roles linked norms and situations, so virtues link character and situations:

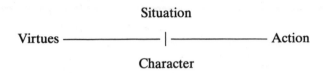

Situation

Virtues ——————— | ——————— Action

Character

Knowing what virtues are important, therefore, may provide some guidance for action. First, it helps us to know *what to look for* in the situation and *which features of the situation* are crucial. The importance of discernment emerged early in our discussion. In order to make the right decision, the actor must discern those aspects of the situation that are morally relevant. We indicated that these aspects will have to do with features in the situation that impact on the fulfillment of prima facie duties. We also indicated that being in a professional position might be morally relevant, but that its relevance rests in the total complex of expectations that attach to the professional role. These, as we have seen, have a lot to do with character.

Now we are in a position to refine this analysis a bit further. While all prima facie duties are important, and all aspects of the situation that impact on their fulfillment count, the most important aspects of a situation may be those that have to do with key virtues. Since fidelity emerged as a central virtue for professionals, the aspects of the situation that are most important for Ruth are those that have to do with fidelity, or being trustworthy. The key will be to discern what actions in the situation establish trust and what actions have the potential for violating trust.

The Meaning of Our Acts

This need for discernment implies something else that is not always taken sufficiently into account in theories about moral decision making. Two acts can look the same to an external observer, but have very different meaning from the perspective of the person acting.

Suppose Ruth decides to keep confidence. Is this a trustworthy act? Some might think that it is—that she is exercising a professional duty of confidentiality toward her client. But note that she may have decided to keep confidence for very different reasons—e.g., because she does not trust her colleague on the staff, or because it makes her feel important to have a professional crisis for which she alone is responsible. Though the act looks the same to an external observer—information was not divulged—the act does *not* have the same meaning from the internal perspective. In some cases, the act is hardly praiseworthy. Ruth would not be likely to be considered virtuous if she is focusing solely on her own needs or playing power games with her client. Indeed, she would be violating the image of the professional that is urged in professional codes. She would not be proving herself trustworthy.

This is another way of saying that the same act may be done for different *reasons*. To exhibit virtue or integrity, to be honorable, is not merely to do the right thing but is to do it for the right reasons. While any of us might have clues that would help us to guess those reasons, at some level the full meaning of an act is available only to the agent.[6] Only the agent knows what her motives and intentions truly were. As we act, we create meaning by giving expression to certain intentions and by offering—to ourselves, if not publicly—certain reasons and not others for what we do.

There is a sense, then, in which the true meaning of an act is always to some extent a private matter. It depends on the motivations, the situation, and the perception of the actor. The same act can be done for different reasons—and only the actor knows what reasons truly lie behind it. While I can judge another's character as I watch his or her patterns of action, some aspects of character are very private.

Public and Private Meaning

This suggests that trustworthiness requires two additional tasks on the part of the professional. The *private* nature of actions affects the possibilities for being trustworthy in at least two important ways.

First, actions are easily misunderstood by others. Since the same act could arise from different motivations and intentions, there is always the risk that the act will be interpreted differently by the client or public than it is by the professional. When misunderstood, we want to cry out: You can't judge me; you don't know the full reasons for what I did! Such self-defensiveness is understandable, but not laudable. Misunderstanding should be expected, given the private nature of acts. And professionals should be prepared to respond to misunderstanding with trustworthiness—i.e., without retaliating.

The current outcry against professionals is partly a desire for more *public* display of the reasons for what professionals do. Current sentiment includes a refusal to permit professionals alone to determine the meaning of acts. The public can understand and judge better whether actions were truly praiseworthy when reasons are divulged. I applaud this move and will return to it in part III. For the moment, the point is to make clear that the meaning of an act may not appear the same from outside as it does from inside, and that part of the trustworthiness of the professional must be a willingness to bear with the insult and misunderstanding that this multiplicity of meanings can create.

The second danger arises from the private nature of actions: the danger of self-deception. Part of the reason that we should welcome public inspection and more accountability in defining the meaning of our acts is that it is all too easy to deceive ourselves. While on some level only the agent knows the true meaning of her act, the agent may not recognize her true motivations. In the name of love we can do hateful and destructive acts. In the name of beneficence we can justify violations of trust and interferences into the lives of others that really come from our own desire for power.

Jungian psychoanalyst Adolf Guggenbühl-Craig argues that those who try very hard to be helpful often build up negative energy that expresses itself in unintended ways.[7] The "helping" professions are particularly prone to this shadow side of action. Ministers may be attracted into their profession out of a genuine love of people and desire to bring them to God. But lurking underneath it all may be a fascination with sin and with the ugly sides of human life. All professionals are tempted by the power they possess. Think of how important Ruth may feel if she is the only one who knows Kathy's plight—or how tempting it might be to divulge it to a colleague in order to gain praise for how wisely Ruth has acted. Thus, in order to know the full meaning of an act, the professional must be constantly on guard for her hidden agendas.

Once again, being trustworthy goes far beyond simply keeping confidence. It means doing so *for the right reasons*—not out of desire for power or out of need for reassurance, but out of genuine desire to be trustworthy, coupled with an accurate perception of the requirements of the situation. Here is where trustworthiness as a virtue supplements and provides a corrective to simple right action.

The Problem of Perspective

But now it seems as though perhaps we are falling into the trap that Veatch so forcefully wanted to avoid—the problem of special pleading on the part of professionals.[8] We have said that the meaning of the act can be known in some sense only by the person acting. Can professionals now claim exemption from following rules not because of professional status or special duties embodied in professional codes, but because of knowing the true meaning of the act or having the only correct interpretation? Can any act be justified on grounds that it fits my integrity?

This is a danger I want to avoid. The recent rise of liberation theology helps to demonstrate how much of our perspective and vision is distorted by assumptions that we take for granted and have difficulty confronting. We are racist and sexist without knowing it. Similarly, the very process of professional training involves learning to perceive selectively. Indeed, the Cornwall Collective charges that "required courses [in seminary] ensure that the student acquires what the white, male, middle-class decision-makers of the school regard as basic preparation for ministry."[9] Professionals will tend to see things one way, to understand meaning within a certain range of possibilities. This is not necessarily the best way, or the most accurate.

How, then, do we seek a true perspective? How do we know when we are permitting truth to guide our actions, and when we are simply reinforcing our biases?

First, to say that we create meaning as we act, and that to some extent only the actor knows the true meaning of an act, is not to say that we cannot test the appropriateness of an actor's description.[10] Some descriptions of an act are simply not plausible. Some descriptions make no sense given what the agent knows about the circumstances. If I know that a well contains poisoned water, and I draw from it and give a drink to someone, can I honestly claim that I had no intention of poisoning that person? Can I say that I just wanted to satisfy the person's thirst?[11] Such a description seems implausible at best.

Other descriptions are not consonant with what we know of the agent's character—her or his life story. We noted above that sometimes it is difficult to reconcile a proposed action with our image of ourselves. When this happens, it can either push us toward a new self-image, or it can push us to redefine the action. Suppose Ruth breaks confidence. She claims to do so out of a desire to help Kathy. But her colleague knows that Ruth tends to need reinforcement and is uncertain in her judgments. In this case, the colleague might challenge Ruth's description, arguing that it does not match her character or life story.

Second, my description of my action and my definition of my motives are never separable from my story. As I tell my story I give reasons for what I have done. These reasons are meant both to describe and to justify my acts: "I broke confidence because I was afraid she would commit suicide." As Joan Didion puts it, we live by the imposition of a story on the disparate events of our lives.[12]

But my story is always formed in response to a community and its story.[13] Different virtues—different ways of perceiving and responding and describing the reasons for what we do—are encouraged by different communities.[14] Hence, whom I try to be is always in part a question of the validity of the story of my community and of my part in continuing and challenging that story. Whether one is a defender of the system or a practitioner of civil disobedience, to some extent the meaning of one's actions will depend on the story provided by the community and its ways of perceiving and interpreting the world.

Our individual stories may also be judged by their coherence with the stories of our communities, therefore. Indeed, Hauerwas suggests that the individual's acts must be compatible with the "narrative embodied in the language used" to describe the act.[15] To unpack this cryptic sentence a bit, what is at stake here is the way in which the moral notions that we use to interpret situations—the language forms that we bring—are already the product of a community. If Ruth claims that she wants to do the *loving* thing, she cannot claim just any meaning for *love*. The meaning of this term is given in part by the history of the community and its use of the term. Thus, if we urge clergy to use specifically theological language, as Menninger does, their actions will have to be compatible with the community stories implied by that language.

And, of course, the stories of the community must also be judged for their adequacy in providing a moral framework and for their truthfulness.

What are the criteria for an adequate or "true" story? A leading proponent of the "story" approach to ethics, Hauerwas proposes at least the following criteria:[16]

—A true story should have the power to release us from destructiveness;
—It should provide a way of seeing through our current distortions;
—It should have room to keep us from having to resort to violence;
—It should have a sense for the tragic, for how meaning transcends power.

These criteria are minimal. Others could be added.[17] But even with these minimal criteria, the limits of some cultural stories are immediately apparent. Racist and sexist stories do not provide ways of seeing through current distortions. Stories that offer trust in technological power do not provide an adequate sense for the tragic in human life.[18] Stories that require professionals never to err may lead to violence and the violation of the basic norms of respect for the client. And so on.

Stories and the Story

Professional groups often have a dominant story embedded in their language—e.g., a story of the search for truth, or of the way in which justice comes about only by balancing conflicting claims before an impartial tribunal. Individual practitioners' stories can be judged in part by how much of these dominant group stories they incorporate. But probably no professional group has so clear and so dominant a story as do clergy. Ministers in Christian churches judge their stories by the gospel story. This story meets the criteria above, and it becomes the standard for judging actions.

For example, we suggested in chapter 5 that the theological concept of betrayal might be important to a professional who is struggling with the meaning of faithfulness and with ways of finding faithful action. But betrayal is not simply a theological *concept*. It is embodied in *stories*, particularly the story of Judas. To judge our stories by the gospel story means in part to look for the ways in which my action reflects Judas rather than Jesus. Our stories can be judged by how they fit with and are illumined by the stories that give coherence to our community of faith.

This has sometimes led ministers—and their congregations—to think that clergy should imitate or try to be like Jesus.[19] I disagree. To put one's own story next to the Story is *not* the same as a simple ethic of imitating Christ. The normative power of a story should not be confused with imitating what someone did. There is no simple way to recreate the setting

102

in which Jesus or Judas acted, or to emulate or avoid particular actions. What we need to derive from the gospel stories is not lists of actions to recreate in our lives, but approaches that help us understand *how to interpret* what happens and what the true meaning of our action is.[20]

Take, for example, the parable of the good Samaritan.[21] As we listen to this story, it is all too tempting to think that the point of it is tell us to *be like the good Samaritan*—to help those who are injured, to give succor to our neighbor without thought of recompense, and so on. In short, we are tempted to turn the story into a series of rules or a set of behaviors to imitate. It sounds like a perfect statement of the rule of beneficence. And all too often it is preached this way.

But this is not the point of the parable. The parable is told in answer to the question, Who is my neighbor? The original audience to whom it was addressed were Jews. They would have been expected to identify *not* with the Samaritan, but with the injured Jew lying by the side of the road. From this perspective, the question addressed by the parable is neither, Who is the neighbor whom I should help? nor How do I help my neighbor? but, Who is my neighbor when I am in need of help?

The point of the parable is not to tell us how to *act*, but to tell us how to *perceive*. It tells us who our neighbor is. Specifically, it tells us that our enemy is our neighbor. "The power of the parable resides in its symbolic capacity to portend a world in which the enemy is the compassionate one, and one's 'colleagues' reject one."[22] This was a shocking idea in Jesus' day, and it is equally shocking today. To be told that Russians, members of the Ku Klux Klan, or riders with the Hells Angels are not our enemies but our neighbors—and that we may expect to get help from them—is difficult for us to accept.

Biblical stories do not tell us what to do. They tell us something about the perspective from which we should view the world. In this case, the perspective is that of the wounded Jew lying by the side of the road. The meaning of the story goes far beyond simple rules about helping others, therefore. It has to do with vision.

The Virtue of Prudence

And this suggests that there is yet another virtue that should be central for professionals: the virtue of prudence. For prudence has to do with vision or accurate perception.

Now this may come as a bit of a surprise. In a recent book on professional ethics, Darrell Reeck argues for the value of prudence in professional decision making. But he limits prudence to "a due regard for one's own welfare and wisdom in handling one's affairs."[23] And indeed, we often think of prudence in terms of carefulness—a willingness to forgo pleasure today in order to preserve goods for tomorrow, a kind of calculating self-protectiveness that does not squander our goods or resources. Prudence has come to mean a utilitarian weighing of benefits and harms, and a willingness to compromise benefits in order to avoid harms. Caution and circumspection are associated with the prudent person.

But these words appear only in the fourth definition of *prudence* in Webster's![24] The virtue of prudence, classically understood, was not at all this "timorous, small-minded self-preservation."[25] The interpretation that focuses on caution and circumspection is a modern distortion of the meaning of the virtue. It has caused one advocate for social justice to cry out, "Prudence, you have been so disfigured that . . . I almost feel the need to shout, 'Be rash!' "[26]

As Josef Pieper explains, in its original meaning, the virtue of prudence is "the perfected ability to make right decisions."[27] It means letting the truth of real things determine what we do. Prudence is "the ability to govern and discipline oneself by the use of reason."[28] It is thus the virtue associated with discernment: "Perhaps all that has been said about moral discernment in this chapter is only another way of talking about the virtue of prudence."[29] Prudence is thus central to ethical decision making.

Prudence involves both *deciding* (not being irresolute) and *deliberating* (not being impetuous).[30] In an action-oriented society such as ours, we tend to focus on deciding: on doing, acting, taking charge. But equally important to the formation and expression of this virtue is deliberation. Sufficient attention must be given to the truth of real things so that we may perceive what is required. This attentiveness is what will permit the professional to see where the issues of trust lie in the dilemma and how the factors in the situation are to be interpreted and assessed.

Accumulated experience can develop attentiveness. Professionals often rely on their experience in justifying their decisions: "In my experience, this issue will resolve itself if we don't interfere." "My professional judgment is that this drug should not be recommended for this patient." "In all my years of ministry, I've never seen a case where that helped." Such reliance on experience is frustrating for laypeople. It implies that only the professional can make the decision. At its best, however, it points toward the virtue of prudence. Professionals have tended to trust their experience and the wisdom that it brings in order to make right decisions—to be prudent in the sense of perceiving accurately what is required. In this regard, Hulme's charge that experience is devalued in the ministry is a sobering charge: churches may not be encouraging prudence.[31]

But professionals often ignore another prerequisite for prudence. Even more important than experience to the process of deliberation is *silence.* " 'Prudence as cognition' . . . includes above all the ability to be still in order to attain objective perception of reality."[32] This is what ministers do when they pray, presumably! Prayer is meant to be an attitude of openness that permits the truth of real things to impinge on our consciousness, to show us where we might be in error, to make clear what God requires, what is happening, and what the appropriate response is.

Prayer is not an infallible guide, of course. White people have prayed to a "white" God for centuries without perceiving their racist biases; men have prayed to a "male" God without perceiving the sexism that permeates their lives and distorts their social relations and institutions. Thus, prayer itself is limited by cultural distortions. It may be a corrective to some misinterpretations, but it is not a guarantee of accurate perception. Nonetheless, while prayer is not the *only* guide to ethical decision making, it has a place that is not always recognized by those who stress rational decision making alone.

Thus, trustworthiness is not the only virtue for professionals. In addition, the professional needs prudence—accurate perception of the real and willingness to act in accord with that perception. The importance of this virtue will become even more evident in part III.

Summing Up

We have now looked at a second dimension of ethics: questions of character. We saw in chapter 4 that as professionals respond to ethical dilemmas, they are likely to try to *be* something—to embody certain virtues and traits. These are hinted at in professional codes. Two such virtues emerge as central: trustworthiness and prudence. The first has to do with fidelity, and it has been traditionally understood as central to the professional life. But the second is equally important, for it is the virtue that helps us to perceive what is required in the situation—to "act in accord with the real." As we act, we create meaning, we create our own characters, we live a story. In trying to make decisions about what to do, we can therefore also ask, Who am I becoming? What will it mean to my story if I do this? and, Is this consonant with the story that gives guidance to mine? These questions do not provide simple and direct rules for action, but they illumine deeper dimensions of ethical dilemmas. Ruth may very well have a rule that requires her to keep confidence. But as she asks these deeper questions, she will be pushed to consider what actions are consonant with the kinds of virtues she wants to develop as a professional. She will be pushed to consider what actions would be truly trustworthy in the situation.

PART III
STRUCTURE

7. PROFESSIONAL POWER

IN part II, we saw that our approach to ethical dilemmas can be rounded out by asking about virtue and character. Does this action fit the life story that I am trying to build? How does it affect my integrity? How can I be trustworthy here? These are all questions about character that might influence an ethical decision. Thus, we moved from looking at the isolated case or decision toward a perspective that takes seriously the continuity of action and its effects on the agent. As we did so, the virtue of fidelity, or being trustworthy, emerged as a central virtue, to be supported by the virtue of prudence.

But now we must ask, Is virtue enough? Is the trustworthiness or prudence of the professional an adequate protection for the client? Is it sufficient to count on the trustworthy trustee? Is there anything *else* about the professional situation that should be taken into account when making ethical decisions?

I think there is. If we return to the concept of "trustee" once more and this time add the "outside" perspective on the professions, we find that virtue is not sufficient. A careful look at the particular role of the professional trustee will show why depending on the character of the professional is not enough. In this chapter we will look at several forms of trusteeship in order to locate the peculiar power of professionals.

Parents, Professionals, and Friends

Professionals are not the only people who might be said to be in a position of "trusteeship" over others. Parents and friends can also be considered trustees. In each case, the person is entrusted with something valuable. Intimate knowledge that gives power over the other is gained. Both are understood to have strong obligations to be trustworthy and faithful.[1] They are expected to use their powerful knowledge for the good of the other, not for themselves. Like professionals, therefore, parents and friends are given power over something important and are expected in turn to exercise that power in a trustworthy fashion.

And both parenthood and friendship have been used as paradigms or analogies for the professional-client relationship. The similarity between parenthood and professionalism is exemplified by the fact that both are called "paternalistic" relationships.[2] To the extent that the trustee is entrusted with power in order to help another, both parents and professionals would seem to be in a central role of trusteeship. Similarly, friendship is a form of trusteeship: we expose ourselves to our friends, become vulnerable to them, and trust them. Friends are assumed to act with the good of the other in mind—indeed, we often think this is what makes a friendship.

In fact, a number of commentators have used friendship as a model for the professions in general or for ministry in particular. Charles Fried suggests that "the analogy of professional roles to the concept of friendship is striking."[3] Hulme suggests that the minister is a "professional friend";[4] Strain and Southard both use the image of friend in describing the role of minister;[5] and Letty Russell notes that Jesus called us to be "friends" rather than servants.[6] Thus, there is some evidence that friendship might be a form of trusteeship similar to the professional role in general or the ministerial role in particular.

Yet I think there are some important structural differences between parenthood, friendship, and professional practice. These structural differences are morally relevant. Thus, all may be forms of trusteeship, but parenthood and friendship do not provide adequate paradigms for professional ethics.

In all three cases, we are talking about a relationship in which one party becomes vulnerable to another and the other gains power. Thus, the similarity has to do with the issue of vulnerability and power—all three include the use (and possible abuse) of power over a vulnerable person. It is precisely for this reason that the trustworthiness of all three is so highly touted.

Yet there are differences in the type of power gained and the structures in which it can be used. Under ordinary circumstances, the intimacy—and the vulnerability—of the child to the parent is a *natural* intimacy that comes of "being family"—of sharing the same life space, often the same genes, the same food and drink, and to some extent, the same corporate destiny. This kind of natural intimacy is generally lacking in professional practice. Perhaps there was a day when the family doctor was so close as to have some of this natural intimacy. Ministers often strive for a kind of family feeling that will engender such natural sharing and trusting.[7] But under most contemporary conditions of professional care, this is not the case.

The intimacy that arises between professional and client is not the natural intimacy of sharing living space and common necessities through time, but an *imposed* intimacy. It is an intimacy given with some reluctance to secure some end. If I want appropriate medication, I must divulge my aches and pains and submit to prodding and poking. If I want the prayers and comfort of my minister, I must share my troubled spirit. And I must do so no matter who the minister is. Even if Kathy does not like Ruth, so long as she needs the help of a minister, she must divulge her painful position. Personal characteristics of the professional can surely facilitate that sharing, and it is true that we generally have some choice about which professional we see, but there is nonetheless a sense in which we have to share no matter what we think of the person if we want her or his professional services. The parenthood image falters, therefore, because of the forced and unnatural intimacy between professional and client.

Furthermore, the protective mechanism of reciprocal intimacy which generally exists in family and friendship settings is lacking in most delivery of professional care.

111

Professionals see their clients in the office, preserving their private space and not welcoming clients to their homes.[8] The exchange of information is unequal: "The client . . . must tell [the professional] all secrets," but the professional need not tell the client anything.[9] Even ministers, who practice so much in the public eye of their clientele, can usually hide their personal problems while they deal constantly with the personal problems of parishioners. They may choose to share from their personal histories, but the sharing is chosen and controlled by them, not by what the client wants to know. When clients share with professionals, the extent and nature of what is shared are often controlled by the professional. The vulnerability and intimacy that the client is expected to display to the professional take place in an unequal setting and often in an alien environment. Lack of reciprocal vulnerability clearly means that the client lacks some protective mechanisms that might be available to a friend or child—"You can tell on me, but I can't tell on you."

Yet some might argue that these structural differences apply to other professionals but not to ministers. Ministers practice their profession in public, and therefore are vulnerable to their congregations.[10] Thus, there is more reciprocal vulnerability than may be assumed. Further, because ministers are seen not only in an office, but also in other settings, and are involved in the total life of their congregations, the intimacy that develops may seem more natural than it does for other professionals. Thus, perhaps these important structural differences apply to other professionals, but not to clergy.

Power and Authority

However, I think there remains an important structural difference between the professional role of minister and the trusteeships of parents and friends. Professionals practice in an institutional context, girded by laws, social mores, relatively clear role expectations, and groups of other professionals who both support and delimit their spheres. The professional context carries legal and moral sanctions for inappropriate behavior. The existence of explicit codes of morality for professional groups indicates how institutionalized professional practice is.

This institutionalized character leads to a morally relevant difference in assessing the issue of power and vulnerability. As Sissela Bok puts it, confession in institutionalized practices "increases the authority of the listener while decreasing that of the speaker."[11] While all confession lends vulnerability to one and power to another, there is an "added power" lent by the institutional role.[12] The power held by friends is a personal power. If I love my friend and do not wish to lose the friendship, I will do what my friend asks. But my friend has no authority to compel me to do it; her only hold on me is the threat of losing the friendship. Professionals, on the other hand, have an even stronger, though sometimes more subtle, power. As Switzer puts it, "We bring not only the power of a personal presence but also our impact as symbols."[13] The power held by the professional over the client is not simply a personal power. It is a social power.

In sociological language, professionals have not just "power" (the ability to influence my behavior), but "authority" (legitimated and institutionalized power).[14] Professionals represent society and its power in a way that friends do not. "The minister is a physical representation of the whole community of faith, of the tradition, of a way of viewing the meaning of life, . . . and of God."[15] This representative power is called authority. Professionals have authority to put me in jail, to hospitalize me, to excommunicate me, or in other ways to affect significantly the structures of meaning and of freedom in my life. Their power is both legitimated and institutionalized.

To be sure, parents and friends have power. Both parents and friends may change the structures of freedom of my life: they can call the police or the mental health authorities and ask to have me committed. But the actual hospitalization or confinement requires the stamp of professional approval. This is the stamp of authority—of a societal decision exercised through the persona of the professional. It is not the personal qualities of the professional that give her or him this power over others, but the very status of being a professional.[16] Part of the role definition of professionals includes this representative power on behalf of society—this power that is legitimated into authority and girded by institutions.

Hence, professionals have a symbolic and representative power that goes beyond the interpersonal power of friends. Indeed, some have argued that it is not possible for professionals to be friends with their clients without jeopardizing the professional role.[17] The difference between the professional as trustee and parents or friends as trustees, therefore, lies in the type of power held and the setting in which it is exercised. To be vulnerable in an unequal and unnatural setting and in the face of a structured and institutionalized power is the fate of clients. I believe that this constitutes a morally relevant difference from other forms of trusteeship. Even in circumstances where professional groups become vulnerable to public exposure or criticism, and where the sharing of information is more reciprocal, professionals nonetheless retain a morally relevant form of power over their clients.

The Problematics of Power

The public is sensitive to abuses of power on the part of professionals. A professional who takes advantage of the weakness of a client for personal gain will be labeled "unprofessional" or "unethical."[18] But so long as professional power is exercised within the boundaries defined as legitimate for the profession, society has not—until recently—perceived a problem. The fact that professional power is legitimated and institutionalized has tended to blind us to the importance of the mere existence of that power. Precisely because it is legitimate power—authority—we forget that there is a significant power gap between professional and client. We also forget that it is a type of power that is very difficult for clients to overcome. The vulnerability of client to professional

114

differs from the vulnerability of friend to friend: the professional can not only hurt my feelings, but has legitimated, institutionalized power to make significant changes in my life.

Until a decade ago, for instance, Kathy would have needed the sanction of a professional in order to secure an abortion. Abortions were permitted only in restricted cases. And it was physicians who decided which cases "merited" this medical intervention. Their power over her would have been considerable.

In the current legal climate, Ruth clearly has no power to prevent Kathy from having an abortion.[19] Her authority does not extend this far. Nonetheless, she does have considerable power and authority. She represents the church, and she represents God.[20] She is, as Southard puts it, a "spiritual authority."[21] And as such, she is "an evaluator of behavior, an upholder of standards, a mediator of godly acceptance of judgment."[22] She interprets for Kathy how her pregnancy and contemplated abortion are seen in the eyes of the church and in the eyes of God. She can facilitate or obstruct the abortion—e.g., by giving or withholding money. She can shame Kathy or provide support. As a professional minister, she interprets on behalf of the church the meaning—and consequences—of Kathy's act. Indeed, she will do this wittingly or unwittingly: her actions, as well as her words, will provide an interpretation of the meaning and significance of Kathy's plight. All of this is a legitimate part of her professional authority.

Now suppose Ruth is opposed to abortion and considers it a grave sin that threatens Kathy's salvation. She therefore tells Kathy that she is a sinner, in need of repentance, and that she must not take this course of action. To do so is not an abuse of authority as it is generally understood. She has not sought her own personal gain. She has neither violated confidence nor broken any of the rules of her professional code. She appears to be acting within the legitimate boundaries of her professional relationship. In short, she remains a trustworthy trustee, using her skill and knowledge to secure the legitimate ends of her profession. Is there anything wrong with this?

115

The traditional view has been that it is only the abuse of power to secure personal ends that requires watching. So long as the professional does not combine personal interests with professional ones, but stays carefully within the boundaries of legitimated professional goals, the existence of the professional's power is not problematic. Hence, the integrity of the professional person—her or his ability to keep personal agendas out of the professional relationship—was considered a sufficient corrective to problems of professional power.[23]

Edmund Pellegrino, for example, argues that the traditional ethic of integrity and fidelity suffices for the professional's relations with the individual client.[24] Though he calls for a new understanding of the social dimension of ethical problems in the professions, he assumes that integrity (character) and fidelity are a sufficient corrective to any problems of power in the one-to-one relationship.

I disagree. The traditional ethic of integrity and faithfulness is not altogether adequate, even for the interpersonal dimension. It fails to take account of the ways in which the social dimension—the representative nature of the power held by professionals—influences the interpersonal arena. It fails to deal with structural problems in the power gap between professional and client. All too many ministers act precisely as Ruth hypothetically does here, using the vulnerability of the client to secure legitimate professional ends. With the best of intentions, and within the boundaries of professional practice, they impose a definition of reality on the client in ways that are problematic ethically. As Bok puts it, "Institutional practices of self-revelation . . . are also unequalled means for imposing orthodoxy of every kind."[25]

The Power of Definition

Professionals have the power to define reality.[26] And it is this power that makes dependence on individual virtue an insufficient corrective.

Professionals profess. As Everett Hughes puts it, "They profess to know better than others the nature of certain

116

matters, and to know better than their clients what ails them or their affairs."[27] Clients must trust professionals, because they do not have enough knowledge to criticize or judge their work. "This is the essence of the professional idea and the professional claim."[28]

In short, the profession is not only entrusted by society with maintenance of a cultural heritage, but also begins to redefine and shape that cultural heritage. The profession defines how some aspect of society is to be thought of and how policy is to be formulated around it. Ruth draws on her professional training to define how a teenage pregnancy and the possibility of abortion are to be interpreted. She may take it as a sign of sin and an opportunity to require repentance or increase shame. She may take it as an unfortunate mistake and an opportunity to offer forgiveness. Each of these approaches has been used historically by her professional group; each falls within the legitimate boundaries of authority; and each constitutes a definition of reality. As Freidson puts it, "The profession claims to be the most reliable authority on the nature of the reality it deals with. . . . The layman's problem is re-created as it is managed—a new social reality is created by the profession."[29]

Consider, for example, the person with a sore throat who decides to seek "professional help." As Menninger notes,

> If a man with a sore throat or a severe headache were to go to a physician . . . he would be given an examination and then appropriate medication. But suppose the same sufferer were to go to a clergyman. Instead of aspirin or penicillin, he might be given a long interview. In it he might be asked if his headache could reflect preoccupation with a moral conflict, or his sore throat be an expression of regret over bitter words. . . . Some might condemn this minister for presumption, yet there have been many psychosomatic studies which have borne out exactly the implications of these questions.[30]

Is a headache an illness? How is the reality of this phenomenon to be defined? Each profession tends to define the meaning of the symptom differently.

Consider what might have happened to Kathy if she had gone to a doctor with her pregnancy. She would have received advice about abortion procedures (and perhaps about alternatives to abortion) rather than a lecture on sin and an offer to pray for her soul *or* an offer of forgiveness. To use either the language of sin and repentance *or* the language of acceptance and forgiveness is to provide an interpretation of the meaning of her problem. Both construct reality for her.

To be sure, the professions alone do not determine where clients choose to go with their problems. The tendency to go to one professional group over another is reinforced by the media, by symbol systems in the culture, and by popular mythologies. Groups in society can withdraw their trust in a profession—for example, by establishing self-help clinics that ignore traditional medical structures or "house churches" that are outside the structures of denominations. Morris Cogan argues that what makes an occupation a profession—with all the legitimized power that entails—is partly the ability of the occupational group to convince society that it handles problems more efficaciously than other groups do.[31] As Kathy tries to live out her *own* story in such a way as to have integrity, some professional definitions of her problem will seem fitting and some will not. When professional definitions lose their sense of "fit" with people's lives, the profession loses power.

Nonetheless, a significant part of that cultural determination derives from the professions, for they are given the power to define their territories. Homosexuality was once defined as a sickness by the medical profession and universally acclaimed a sin in the church; it no longer is. Numerous phenomena that were once considered sins are now either crimes or diseases—e.g., alcoholism, drug addiction, antisocial behavior. As Menninger puts it, "The distinction between sin, symptom, and crime *is* the professional management the subject receives—i.e., what rescuer is chosen."[32] Perhaps the most striking (and amusing) example of the power of professional definition is the complete reversal of medical opinion on masturbation during the last century. A hundred years ago, masturbation was a disease that could cause all sorts of ill effects; it is now a cure that can cause all sorts of good effects![33]

In short, professionals do not simply fix problems; they also define them. In the early 1970s, when prenatal diagnosis was becoming an established medical technique, physicians began to declare that certain groups of women needed this technique.[34] They defined a new need in society, and changed the nature of the experience of pregnancy for many women. When we remember that professions deal with basic issues of human life such as relations to nature, others, and God, we begin to understand the tremendous power of definition possessed by the group that is given professional status.

Such power is reinforced by the autonomy of the profession. One of the distinguishing marks of professions is their freedom to determine the proper boundaries of their work and how it should be conducted. Only those within the profession are presumed able to censure their colleagues for inappropriate work.[35] The structures of professional practice thus reinforce the power to define reality. The gap in power that would derive simply from the acquisition of specialized and esoteric knowledge or skill is reinforced by the self-control and autonomy given to professionals to direct their work.

Clergy Power and Authority

If this is true for all professions generally, it is even more true for clergy. The primary role of clergy is rarely defined as "the social construction of reality" or "defining reality." Yet that is precisely what clergy do. Other professionals offer definitions of reality under the cover of doing something else. For instance, under the guise of providing medical care, the physician interprets the symptoms and complaints presented by the patient: "You have an ulcer and must change your diet." The interpretation is subsumed under the goal of treatment; it is therefore subtle and sometimes difficult to discern.[36]

119

To a large extent, however, the clergy have as a primary role the provision of an appropriate language with which to define the meaning of human experience. This language sometimes seems archaic—"sin," "redemption," "reconciliation." Yet, as Menninger and Hauerwas argue, it may be important to retain that specialized language, for it is a clue to a meaning system.[37]

One woman minister advocates "the necessity of presenting images of faith that allow the hearers to reframe their experience of the world in the light of God's saving activity."[38] Others agree: "The facts do not have the last say. There is a reality of 'feast' beyond the facts as we perceive them";[39] "The naming and transforming of images and symbols of the spiritual dimensions of our lives is integral to seeking wholeness."[40] Or, as another minister put it, "Things are not as they appear to be, says the Christian. Part of the ministry is to help people see that God always works under the surface in a hidden fashion."[41] What all of these commentators are saying is that the naming of reality is central to the task of ministry. The minister does not simply heal or help or console. She defines reality by offering a new language, a perspective on hidden meanings, a transformation of ordinary symbols, a hope in the midst of seeming hopelessness. Part of the task of the minister is to "speak the truth."[42] This "truth" is the truth formed by theological language and given shape in the community of faith. In "telling the story," clergy are often providing the framework by which our own stories can be judged and interpreted. The social construction of reality is at the heart of the minister's vocation.

And this does put clergy in a different position from other professionals. One of the criticisms leveled against professionals today is that in defining reality they touch upon value issues that exceed the legitimate goals and boundaries of their professions. For example, Bayles argues that the superior knowledge or expertise of professionals does not qualify them "to make value choices significantly affecting a client's life plans or style."[43] Yet it is precisely this matter of making value choices that is integral to the practice of ministry. The minister "is expected to be an evaluator of behavior."[44] The minister is considered a moral authority whose pronouncements carry moral weight. Or, as one person put it, "The minister's visit symbolizes *the judgment*."[45] This means that ministers are involved in defining moral reality even as they invite the parishioner into the office.

Fidelity and the Limits of Professional Power

In such a setting, to say, Trust me, I'm a professional, is to enhance the power gap. The notion that professionals are trustworthy *reinforces* the power gap, though it is intended (as noted in part II) to make professionals accountable. The image of the professional as altruistic and not interested in self-gain works to undermine any suspicion the client might have about the amount or type of power that professionals attain. Precisely because Kathy has gone to a professional she may not be inclined to challenge any definition given to her problem.

Indeed, we want professionals to have power: power to heal, power to litigate, power to set things right with God or nature or other human beings. We purposefully give professionals legitimated power: authority. But with it comes the power to define our needs and problems as well as to respond to them. And with the power of definition comes a significant control over our lives. We want to be able to trust professionals to use this power wisely. And we want them to use it for our own good. But we must not forget that professional definitions of reality are only as good as the state of the art in the profession. What was once a sickness no longer is. What was once a sin no longer is. This suggests that even professional groups have corrected their own previous definitions. Who will watchdog the current definitions?

In *The Making of a Psychiatrist,* David Viscott describes a case in which a woman complained of serious hip pain. A series of psychiatrists told her that she was simply using her hip to release aggression toward her husband, and that there was no reason she could not get up and walk. Viscott describes the day that they finally took an X-ray and discovered that her hip was in fact broken:

> I learned that no matter how well the logic of my discipline explained the emotional meaning of a patient's symptom, I could not be sure that what I understood so well was everything there was to know. . . . Because we saw through her emotional symptoms so easily no one thought to investigate further to see if there were anything physically wrong with her.[46]

Not all cases are this dramatic. But it is true that professionals learn certain ways of seeing problems—and at the same time learn not to see problems in other ways. In the process of professionalization into the medical world, young students eventually begin to adopt the "clinical perspective," emphasizing some data and screening other data out.[47] Thus, by the time one is a practicing professional, her or his perspective is deeply embued with the perspective reinforced by the profession—and with its limits.

C. Wright Mills, Roland Warren, and others demonstrate that most professionals will see problems in individualized terms.[48] They see problems as being located in *people,* not in structures. Even if Ruth does not interpret Kathy's pregnancy as a problem of sinfulness that requires repentance, she is likely to see it in terms of interpersonal difficulties between Kathy and her boyfriend and family. She is far less likely to raise questions about the structures of society and their impact on the unfortunate teenager. Have the limitations and expectations placed on women in our society played a role in Kathy's response to her sexuality?[49] What might the lack of adequate jobs for teenagers have to do with Kathy's feeling that abortion is the only option? Most professionals are not trained to ask these questions. Like most professionals, Ruth will *tend* to perceive the problem on an individual level, not on a corporate or structural level.

Professionals wield tremendous power—the power to define reality. Yet their definitions will be limited by cultural bias and professional training. Relying on individual virtue as a corrective is not sufficient. Some norms for professional behavior are needed that can provide a corrective to ideology. It is to these that we turn in the next chapter.

8. JUSTICE
AND LIBERATION

SEEN not from the inside but from the outside, professions appear to be characterized not by integrity, but by power. Professionals have legitimized power, called authority—authority to affect the meaning of our lives in serious ways, including the power to affect how we will understand and interpret what happens to us.

Traditionally, this power has been understood to be checked in two ways. First, the fiduciary relationship of the professional to the client is considered to limit professional power: the power is to be used *for* the client, not for the professional's personal gain.[1] As we have seen, codes of ethics for professionals stress the honesty, confidentiality, and service orientation of the profession and its practitioners. The professional, as we saw above, is to be the trustworthy trustee. In short, professional character and integrity have been thought to provide a check on the "powerful knowledge" of the professional.

The second check on professional power is the notion of professional indebtedness to society. The trustworthy trustee is *en*trusted with power: power is given, and it can be taken away. If the professional's relationship to society is seen as a matter of *en*trusting of power, then the professional will be bound by obligations to society. The practice of professional skills—and the help given to clients—is therefore not merely a matter of largesse or philanthropy. It is really a matter of justice—of repaying a debt. Thus, B. B. Page and others stress what is "owed" to society by professionals.[2] This is another way of putting a check on the power of professional groups.

Yet, as we have seen, these traditional checks and balances are not adequate. They do not account for some of the biases built into professional perspectives.

Against Professional Autonomy

Indeed, as Howard Moody indicated more than ten years ago, "There is a rising rebellion across the land, undermining every professional royalty and putting question marks under many of our claims to authority and knowledge."[3] Moody linked this rebellion precisely to the existence of power within the professions. He claimed that "professionalism" was being used as a mask ("role" or "persona") to "manipulate, control, and denigrate the abilities and powers of human beings to know and to share what is best for them."[4] The very power of definition which emerged as central for professional groups seems to be the locus of a growing opposition to professions and professionals.

Today, Moody is joined by a host of commentators who rail against the power arrogated by professionals. In a recent essay, philosopher Michael Bayles counters the traditional arguments that have been used to support the need for autonomy in the professions.[5] To the argument that professionals must practice autonomously because only they have sufficient expertise to make decisions, Bayles responds that gross abuses are obvious to anyone. Furthermore, he notes that value judgments enter even into so-called expert decisions. Since values are involved, he argues that laypeople should be included in the decision making. Bayles also suggests that there is no reason that laypeople cannot be involved in judging the organization of the delivery of professional care.

As noted earlier, Lisa Newton also attacks the autonomy of the professions. She indicates that "the heart of the traditional professional ethics was the professional autonomy of the practitioner, accountable to no outsiders."[6] It is precisely this autonomy and lack of accountability that Newton challenges. She argues that the increasing dependence on scientific method within the professions implicitly opens up the question of veracity of professional judgment: anyone sufficiently trained to use scientific method can corroborate or disprove a so-called professional opinion. Thus, there is increasing pressure to make knowledge available to all. As these changes occur, Newton suggests that professionals should not carry virtually unlimited status or authority. They should be "legally empowered to contract for certain services in accordance with their functional qualifications."[7] No longer will traditional "professionals" have unfettered authority; rather, they will have only so much authority as their (demonstrable) expertise merits and as they are given in a specific contract. (This is reminiscent of the "engineering" model proposed by Veatch.) Furthermore, anyone who can demonstrate the requisite "functional qualifications" would be a "professional" on the matter. In a similar vein, Russell argues that the functions of proclaiming the Word and presiding over the sacramental life of the church do not of necessity reside in an ordained—professional—clergy.[8] In the long run, under both proposals there would no longer be a group of persons called "professionals" but only "an ongoing dialogue" in which all who are interested may participate.[9]

Not all would agree with this rather radical conclusion. But Newton, Russell, Bayles, and Moody voice an opposition to professional autonomy which is a constant theme in today's emerging criticism of professions.

New Wine in Old Wineskins

This opposition gets heightened when we look at the question from the perspective of groups that have traditionally been denied entrance into the professions and hence have been underrepresented in them. Women and members of minority groups have particular reason to challenge both the autonomy of the professions and their lack of accountability to society at large.

As Beverly Harrison and Robert Martin argue, the process of professional training into the ministry may not be "good for any woman's health."[10] The "professional" model applied to ministry eroded other models—e.g., the charismatic[11]—in which women were represented in greater numbers. Where ministry was defined in terms of witness to God's presence, women were accepted as evangelists, preachers, and healers. But where a "professional" view took hold and only those with seminary training were permitted to practice ministry, women were excluded from the profession. As Barbara Harris notes, throughout this century women have remained "a tiny, isolated minority in all of the learned professions."[12] Many denominations did not ordain women until the last decade, and as of 1980 women made up only about 3 percent of the clergy population.[13]

Although women are now entering seminary in greater numbers than ever before (women comprise nearly 50 percent of the student body in some institutions), increased numbers alone do not suffice to ensure that traditional patterns of professionalization will be broken, or that women will be truly represented in the profession. Harrison and Martin warn:

> From our perspective the real danger is that women's presence in theological education will be domesticated, successfully channeled into patterns of business as usual in the uncritical work of reinforcing existing patterns of professionalization.[14]

Similar warnings are issued by the Cornwall Collective—a group of women seminary students and ministers who reflect on the struggles of women in seminary education.[15]

The autonomy traditionally granted to professional groups and their lack of accountability to society mean that there is little check and balance not only on the power to grant entrance into the profession but also on the power to define what it means to be an adequate professional. So long as the definitions are drawn from the traditionally dominant group, the social construction of reality will reflect the biases of that group.

127

Thus, there are crucial issues to be dealt with in looking at the distribution and use of professional power. The question is not simply whether the individual practitioner abuses the individual client. The question is also whether the social construction of reality provided by the profession is one that adequately reflects the needs and interests of society, or whether it perpetuates biases and unjust structures. As Letty Russell and other feminists point out, oppression and injustice need not be deliberate. Systemic oppression "arises from interaction of various elements comprising a social system."[16] Here, educational structures, reward systems in work settings, and other aspects of the system combine to create injustice. Depending on professional character is not sufficient, for "the elimination of oppression requires not just reform and change in individual persons, but new rules for society."[17]

Power, Justice, and Liberation

All of this suggests that ethical issues related to the existence, use, and abuse of power should be at the core of an analysis of professional ethics. Yet while sociologists have long touted the autonomy and power of the professions, most ethical analyses have ignored this dimension and focused more narrowly on issues of trust. For instance, Sissela Bok argues that deception is akin to force or violence.[18] She thus hints that analyses of power would be relevant for making decisions about truth telling. Yet in presenting and refuting arguments for lying, she fails to develop any explicit norms in response to the implications of this kinship between deception and power.

Nonetheless, Bok does give us a helpful beginning point. She suggests that we should look at lies from the perspective of the one who is deceived rather than from the perspective of the one who tells the lie.[19] This focuses attention on the question of whose perspective on the situation should be taken as definitive. It suggests that the one against whom power is used has the more accurate perspective on the situation.

Now this is a startling suggestion in a professional context. Since professionals profess—that is, claim to know what is wrong and what to do about it—to suggest that someone else's perspective is more accurate is to turn the tables upside down. Yet this may be precisely what we need if we are to take seriously the questions of power that arise in a professional setting. The power of definition described in chapter 7 raises serious questions about perspective. I do not want to argue that the client's perspective is always right. But I do want to argue that the task for the professional is not simply one of helping the client. The professional must seek to share power and redistribute it.

To put power into the central focus of ethical concern is to argue for the importance of the norm of *justice*. From a biblical perspective, justice includes both correcting imbalances in power and addressing the effects of imbalances in power.[20] Using the jubilee concept of justice, Russell proposes that the experience of jubilee comes to us in "release from the facts of bondage through national deliverance, achievements of equal rights and justice, or personal freedom from a dehumanizing situation."[21] Thus, from a biblical perspective, justice involves the liberation of those who are oppressed.[22] Similarly, the Cornwall Collective points out that the theological language of liberation differs from that of reconciliation in its practical import: it is the appropriate language where justice, concern for class interests, ideologies, and power imbalances are central.[23] If power is central to professional ethics, then justice and liberation become central norms. Liberation means not merely freedom from sin but also freedom from oppressive structures, mythologies, and personal relations.

To put justice and liberation at the heart of professional ethics is quite different from the usual view. In the usual view, the dominant norm for professionals is beneficence—doing good for the client. Most ethical dilemmas are seen as a conflict between beneficence and some other norm, such as truth telling or keeping confidence. In the case of Ruth and Kathy, for instance, the dilemma appears to exist because beneficence and keeping confidence conflict with each other. Ruth must choose one or the other of these norms. Nowhere does justice or liberation appear to be central to the dilemma. The usual view assumes that the trustworthy professional is the one who works for the client's good.

In contrast, the Cornwall Collective urges professional women not simply to mirror the "benevolent" practices of society.[24] In a similar vein Brita Gill urges that pastoral counseling must involve consciousness-raising about issues of power and should not be oriented simply toward helping people adjust to current cultural expectations.[25] She also warns against a "beneficence" that leaves the client indebted rather than liberated.[26] And Letty Russell goes so far as to suggest that ordination "should be for the purpose of subverting the 'clergy line.' "[27] We may need a new definition of what it means to be trustworthy: *the trustworthy one is the one who works for a balance of power that could be called justice.*

Pellegrino comes close to this understanding when he argues that we need a new humanistic basis for medical practice rooted not in the presumed authority of the profession but in "the existential nature of illness and in the *inequality* between physician and patient intrinsic to that state."[28] He does not take for granted that inequality between physician and patient will always exist and must not be questioned. Nor does he assume that the task of the physician is to use her greater power to help the patient. Instead, Pellegrino suggests that the power imbalance between the two must become in some way the root of a new medical ethic. He elaborates as follows:

> Particular features of illness diminish and obstruct the patient's capacity to live a specifically human existence to its fullest. These features create a relationship of inherent inequality between two human beings: one a physician, the other a patient. That inequality must be removed as fully as possible before the humanity of the patient can be restored. The obligation to restore the patient's humanity is intrinsic in the

relationship physicians assume when they "profess" medicine. Specific obligations are derived from the "profession."[29]

In brief, Pellegrino argues that the first priority of a professional ethic must be restoration of the autonomy of the client and liberation of the client from conditions of unequal power.

Liberation and the Importance of Structures

Now there are two paradoxes here. First, liberation cannot be "given" to another.[30] Pellegrino comes dangerously close to the trap of paternalism when he suggests that the physician must "restore the patient's humanity." If the professional does it to the client, or gives it to the client, then it is still the paternalistic model at work. When a client is a passive recipient of a professional's beneficence, then the client is not liberated or autonomous, but is simply receiving help.

Darrell Reeck and others have proposed a central norm of "enabling" the client.[31] This again is close to a liberation model. Yet "enablement" can suggest something that the professional does to (or gives to) the client. Again, one must be careful not to subsume a paternalistic approach of beneficence under the label of empowerment or enablement.

True liberation suggests a model that asks not, How can I help this person? but, How will liberation happen here? How can I be a catalyst in the process? This may seem a subtle shift, but it can have serious ramifications.

For instance, if Ruth asks, How can I help Kathy? she implicitly suggests that she knows what Kathy needs. Thus, she might decide that parenthood is too large a burden for any adolescent, and that the best thing to do is to secure the abortion that Kathy has requested. Note that even if she succeeds in helping Kathy to have an abortion, Ruth continues the imbalance of power. She is in control, making the decisions. The very first decision that she makes involves the power of definition: she defines what Kathy's problem is, and then decides on the proper solution. Even if she "enables" Kathy to secure an abortion, Kathy is not truly liberated.

Now suppose Ruth asked instead, How will liberation happen here? First, she would have to ask what liberation might mean for a frightened teenager. Then she would have to assess what role she plays in Kathy's oppression: Is Ruth, perhaps inadvertently, part of the system that has created a problem for Kathy? And what is the real problem? Is it the fact that Kathy does not have resources to secure an abortion? Or is it the fact that there is very little structural support for Kathy to be a pregnant teenager? How does Kathy perceive the situation? How does she define her needs and problems? Ruth will have to begin by looking very carefully at Kathy's values and life story, rather than at her own professional assessment of teenage parenthood.

While these comments are only suggestive of the path that Ruth might take, they do indicate some initial differences in the meaning of taking liberation seriously as a norm for professional practice. A liberation perspective begins to provide a corrective to the power that professionals have to define or construct reality for the client.

The Importance of Structures

The second paradox lies in the fact that the very structures of professional care tend to put the client in a peculiar position of vulnerability and exposure. Such a position is contrary to what we now see as the first obligation of the professional—the obligation to empower the client, enhance autonomy, and close the power gap. It is possible that the structures under which professional care is given undermine the enactment of this obligation. This is certainly true under the worst of circumstances, but it can also be true under the best of them.

For example, suppose a woman experiences pain with urination. She calls for an appointment at a medical clinic. Three busy signals and two "holds" later, she is asked what the problem is. Either she must share her medical problem with the telephone operator or risk not getting an appointment.

Thus, the very structure of making an appointment violates the presumed confidentiality of physician and patient. And when she arrives for the appointment, the receptionist once again asks, "What's the problem?" Another violation of confidence has occurred.

But now comes the worst violation. The receptionist directs the woman to go—through the crowded waiting room—to the laboratory window, get a urine bottle, take it—back through the crowded waiting room—to the lavatory, fill it, and return it—back through the crowded waiting room. This the woman does, under the watchful eyes of at least twenty people. In such a context, to talk about medical confidentiality in terms of what the *physician* does with this woman's medical record is ludicrous.

The same is true in numerous professional settings. Things that we take for granted about the setting—the teacher stands at the front of the class, the physician is dressed while the patient is naked, the preacher stands *up* in a pulpit and preaches *down* to the congregation—already have an impact on the vulnerability of clients and the power balance in a professional setting.[32] Even the architecture can have its impact, as the placement of the women's lavatory demonstrates.

Professional ethics is not simply a matter of my individual contact with clients, therefore. Other structures enter in, welcome or not. A student who has just received threatening notices from the school financial office has great difficulty hearing anything said in class. A parishioner may hesitate to see a minister if access to the minister's office is too heavily guarded by secretaries, or if the office itself seems insufficiently private.[33] The layout of an office can affect a person's sense of privacy and dignity, and hence can affect his or her ability to be autonomous.

In short, seemingly external structures impact on professional practice every day. They enhance or undermine client autonomy, augment or reduce problems in the distribution of power. Hence, a professional who takes liberation and justice seriously must examine and alter the structures of professional care. Structural change is essential. If questions of power and liberation are at the core of professional ethics, then the professional is bound *by obligations to the client* to work for liberating structures in the delivery of professional services.

This means that the prophetic role of pointing out "the meaning of all the forces at work in the social structure"[34] is required by the pastoral role. A concern for issues related to the structure and delivery of care is *not* a peripheral concern to be relegated only to some professionals or to politicians and social strategists. Nor is it a secondary concern, to be attended to only after the client's needs are satisfied.[35] It becomes an integral part of what is owed by the professional to the client in the trustee role. As feminists declare that the personal is political and the political personal, so we see that attention to the political is necessary as part of care for the personal. To be a trustee is not simply to be entrusted with a portion of a cultural tradition—it is also to be entrusted with the structures in which that tradition is maintained and transmitted.

Suppose, for example, a nursing care facility has different levels of care available, from ambulatory through moderate to intensive care. Normally, as the condition of a patient worsens, he or she is moved through these levels, ending up in intensive care. A panel consisting of a physician, a nurse, a social worker, and the local minister is formed to make judgments about which patients should be moved "up" when beds are emptied. The panel no doubt has every good intention of respecting the autonomy of patients and doing what is best for them. But note that unless the members of the panel pay attention to structures, they may not realize that the pressure to fill empty beds is a powerful force. Since the patients will "end up there eventually anyway," the structures of care seem to indicate that they might as well be moved sooner rather than later. Hence, an ambulatory patient who is beginning to show signs of deterioration may be moved directly to intensive care to avoid the bother of moving him or her twice.[36]

It may be harder to see how these kinds of questions would apply to the individualized counseling case of Ruth and Kathy. But they are just as relevant. What structures in the church serve to reinforce the power of the professional and to heighten the vulnerability of the client? How are offices arranged in the church? Is it necessary to tell a secretary what you want before you can see the minister? Does the minister sit behind a (large, imposing) desk, while the parishioner sits exposed, nervous knees knocking openly? Even the trappings of professional life—the books and files, the diplomas on the wall—can serve to make the one person seem important while the other seems naked and unprotected. Even the clothing worn can make a difference. Clothing for professionals (the physician's coat, the pulpit robe) tends to be protective and concealing. Thus, even their dress may indicate their relative invulnerability and power.

Once power is understood to be a central and defining characteristic of professions, the question of distribution and use of power becomes a central ethical issue. Liberation and justice become primary ethical obligations for the professional. Traditional professional ethics is not adequate because it does not take sufficiently into account the nature and structure of institutions, or the implications of the power gap between professional and client. Nowhere do traditional codes of professional ethics take adequate account of these ethical obligations. The words *justice* and *liberation* do not appear in professional codes of ethics. And while such codes stress the integrity and trustworthiness of the professional, these concerns are rarely if ever linked with attention to the structures of delivery of professional care. Traditional professional ethics has operated from the base of professional autonomy and from an individualized professional-client relationship, rather than from a base of examination of structural and institutional aspects of the delivery of care.[37] To take seriously the impact of structures and institutions on professional ethics will require intensive study of the forms of professional practice in different professions. We shall explore some of these briefly in chapter 9.

Summing Up

Beginning with a perspective that takes seriously the authority of professionals—their distinctive power—we have concluded that two new norms are necessary for professional conduct: justice and liberation. These are norms that take seriously imbalances in power as well as structural realities of professional practice. While the virtues of trustworthiness and prudence are important for professionals, depending on individual integrity is not enough. "Good" people still work within systems. And as Emmet argues, more and more ethical dilemmas may have to do with the nature and structure of systems and institutions, not with individual decisions made by practitioners in a face-to-face encounter with clients.[38]

But where others, e.g., Pellegrino, would argue that the traditional professional ethics is still adequate for face-to-face encounters, I have argued that it is not. The power and authority of the professional impact on the face-to-face encounter. Hence, even an adequate view of ethical decision making in that encounter needs to look carefully at the meaning of professional power and the issue of distribution of power. This in turn requires that we ask two questions not usually understood to fall within the purview of professional ethics: (1) How would liberation happen here? and (2) What would be a just structure for the delivery of professional care?

It is primarily to the second of these questions that we turn in the next chapter. To take seriously the impact of structures and institutions on professional ethics requires a study of the forms of practice in different professions. The lawyer who works in a large law firm is in a very different position from the small-town doctor who works alone in an office. The minister working as an associate on a team is in yet a different position. Structural aspects of professional practice create what I call a "paradox of power" for many professionals, particularly for clergy.

9. POWER AND PARADOX

IN chapter 7 we saw that professionals have a particular type of power—authority. With authority comes the power to define and construct reality. The nature of this power is such that traditional safeguards, such as depending on the virtue of trustworthiness, are not sufficient. Instead, two new norms are needed as central to professional ethics: liberation and justice. These were elaborated a bit in chapter 8.

Part of what gives professionals their authority is the structures and institutional sanctions that surround their work. But as we shall see, these structures not only *give* professionals power, but also *limit* what the individual practitioner can do. It might be more accurate to say that the *professions* wield the power to define reality for society, and that individual practitioners within a profession are then bound by the perspectives and structures that undergird the profession itself. They are also bound by general structures in society that distribute power, and may have more or less power depending on those structures.

There are paradoxes involved in professional power, then: professionals are both powerful and powerless. It is to these paradoxes that we turn attention in this chapter.

Powers and Principalities

Structures and systems have their own reality and they can limit what a person does. To put it starkly, being a "good" person does not change the system. While the system in general gives professionals considerable power, it also binds them in such a way that they are less powerful than we might think at first.

For example, a study of professional women who became newspaper editors showed that many of them continued to think of other women in stereotypical ways. While they were interested in politics, they thought of women in general as being interested only in fashion, clothing, and food—typical "woman's page" fare. Why did they continue to perpetuate these stereotypes even as their own lives exemplified new models? Gaye Tuchman argues that the process of professionalization encountered in their work undermined their ability to identify with other women. "It is difficult for women employees to resist ideas and attitudes associated with success in their profession even if those ideas disparage women."[1]

In short, in order to succeed in their profession, they had to conform to stereotypical thinking about women, while their own lives belied that very thinking! The pressures of the professional work setting and the power of peers and colleagues to define reality inhibited them from pushing for other images of women or from identifying the needs of other women with their own needs and interests. The result in this case was the perpetuation of stereotypes for women in general, even as individual professionals broke out of stereotyped roles in their own lives.

Women who become executives and then perpetuate images denigrating other women are not "bad" people. They are simply responding to and exhibiting the sexism that is structured into their profession.[2] The socialization process, both during professional training and also during the practice of the profession, provides a powerful forum in which the profession as a whole impacts on the perspective of individual practitioners.[3] Depending on the integrity of the individual practitioner to counter distortions in the social construction of reality is not sufficient, for these pressures can be structured in so subtly that most are not aware of their impact.

Moreover, these subtle limiting factors are evident not only in the socialization into a profession, but in the everyday structures of work. Sociologist Eliot Freidson claims that work settings are very important determinants of behavior. He contends that there are organized pressures built into all situations and that what people do "is *more* an outcome of the pressures of the situation they are in than of what they have earlier 'internalized.' "[4] Indeed, he suggests that "there is some very persuasive evidence that 'socialization' does not explain some important elements of professional performance half so well as does the organization of the immediate work environment."[5] If Freidson is correct, depending on the attitudes and values of professionals is not at all sufficient to guarantee ethical behavior, for behavior will be more determined by immediate structures than by the development of professional ideals, character, and images.

Other studies support this view. In a study of nurses serving in different parts of a community hospital, Rose Laub Coser found that the immediate work environment effected serious differences in everything from behavior to professional self-image.[6] She attributes these differences to the different structures in which the nurses worked. On one ward, the goal was to return patients to the community; hence, even small tasks such as filling out release forms could gain importance. On the other ward, that goal was lacking and the same chores were seen merely as bothersome. The group that was praised for not calling physicians learned not to call physicians! And that group developed considerably less sense of themselves as professionals. Hence, though all had received the same professional training, the structures and settings in which they worked, including very specific factors such as systems of reward, led to very different self-images and very different behavior.

Professional training, images, and ideals therefore do not suffice to ensure professional performance in accord with norms and virtues written into codes. While the inside view of the professions might think personal integrity sufficient, the outside view demonstrates that it is not. Attention must also be paid to the work setting. This setting affects not only the power balance between professional and client, but also the ways in which the professional will be likely to interpret events and respond to them.

For example, Ruth will be more or less tempted to divulge confidence depending on her setting and its rewards. What is her relationship with her superior? Is she rewarded for working on her own or for sharing with her colleague? Is she supported professionally?

Taking parish ministry as a model, we shall look at how the structures of work affect professional practice. A similar analysis could be done for any other professional group. The purpose of the analysis is to locate those features in the structures that confine professionals, limiting or augmenting their exercise of power and hence affecting the interpretation and resolution of ethical dilemmas.

The Church as a Voluntary Organization

Studies of ministry over the last two decades have amply documented the multiple problems of role ambiguity and conflict, structural impasse, and failing images of ministers. So pervasive are those problems that Charles Prestwood claims: "If a group of scholars gathered to plan a means of creating a situation in which there would be maximum tension between self-role, role model, and role expectancy, they could devise no more effective structure than that which we find in the ministry today."[7] While this claim was made more than ten years ago, the recent study of the Association of Theological Schools adds a sobering contemporary note when it suggests that "ministers will apparently need to live with a higher degree of tension and ambiguity as the normal way of life."[8]

Here, I shall highlight only a few specific challenges that might affect responses to professional ethical dilemmas. These will be for the most part structural issues that affect the authority of ministers, and hence limit their ability to exercise power.

There is a tremendous gap between the ideal image and the structural realities of ministerial power. James Kennedy relates the ideal that led him into ministry this way:

140

> I clung to my long-held image of . . . preaching the word of
> God with clarity and power to large congregations, and . . .
> ministering with miraculous effectiveness to all of troubled and
> suffering humanity. . . . I mixed my image a bit with touches
> of a knight in shining armor.[9]

Many professionals enter their profession with a touch of the
"knight in shining armor" or some contemporary equivalent.
And no doubt they suffer some disillusionment. Any
unrealistic image is bound to bring disappointments down the
road. But problems are particularly acute in those professions
where the image is one of power and control while the reality,
embodied in structures, is lack of power.

Protestant churches in the United States are voluntary
organizations. If a minister does not please a congregation or
its members, they can leave.[10] Suppose, for example, that
Ruth attempts to offer Kathy a definition of her situation. She
may speak of sin or perhaps of vulnerability; she may raise
questions about whether Kathy is manipulating others; she
may mention the importance of human stewardship and the
Christian affirmation of life as a gift from God. If Kathy does
not like the definition given, she can leave. In theory, the
professional has power to define reality; in practice, that
power is foreshortened by the parishioner's ability to "vote
with her feet."

This is in part because ministers are "generalists" in an age
of specialization.[11] They do not carry the professional prestige
of being the only ones who can counsel adequately or provide
their specific services.

Moreover, the congregation can attempt to have the
minister removed. The specifics of removal differ, of course,
from denomination to denomination. Ministers are protected
better under some forms of polity than under others.
Nonetheless, in most denominations, congregations have
ways of removing problematic clergy. Far from being in
control, therefore, there is a sense in which ministers are at the
mercy of their clientele.[12] They are not so much powerful as
vulnerable—vulnerable to the whims, desires, images, and

expectations of the congregation. The effects of this are widespread—and not always recognized.

One effect is that ministers often try to be relevant to passing trends or fads, to alter their personal style in order to sell themselves more effectively.[13] Personality begins to be at a premium. Where once people went to church because it was church, they now go—or do not go—depending on whether they like the minister's style.

There are serious problems with this trend toward relevance. Popularity contests are rarely won by those who are self-effacing. It is difficult to be selfless and at the same time to have a sufficiently dynamic personality to win congregations. Hence, the structural realities conflict with the traditional image of minister as selfless servant. Success may conflict with an internalized image of the proper role.

Moreover, ministers must often take on new tasks and functions for which they are not well trained. Few enter ministry with a desire to do administrative work: "It is seldom the conscious desire to become a leader in the organizational structure which attracts the young person into the church."[14] Yet one of the realities is that most parish ministers spend the major part of their time doing committee work and administration. Seminaries by and large ignore administration as an area for training of emerging clergy.[15] Most ministers do not value or enjoy administrative work—they rank preaching as the most important of their tasks, and counseling as the most enjoyable, but administration as the most frequent![16] One study showed that 62 percent of the minister's time is spent on the five tasks that are enjoyed the least.[17] It is no wonder that Prestwood charges ministry with being an essentially menial and impotent profession.[18] Even those who cling to some ideals for ministry note the gaps between images of time spent in scholarly study and reflection and the reality of ringing phones and constant crises. With increasing bureaucratization, the same is true for many professionals who enter their professions in order to help others, and soon find themselves buried under a mountain of paperwork.

Aside from limiting the time available for other forms of professional work that are more rewarding to the practitioner, these structural realities exacerbate problems of differing images and expectations. The ATS study amply demonstrates the considerable gaps between clergy and lay expectations: laity are less interested in a learned clergy, do not particularly want their clergy to be politically active or involved, and rank concerns within the parish highest on the list. Clergy worry about continued intellectual growth, are actively concerned for the oppressed, and tend toward a more global vision for the church.[19] In short, as Prestwood puts it, the laity tend toward a "sect" vision that ranks charisma high, while the clergy tend toward a "church" vision that supports a sacramental ministry.[20] The congregation wants a pastor; the minister is likely to see herself as prophet. As Gerald Kennedy puts it, "We are dealing with travelers who will assume that they need a helping hand up the next hill more than they need a revelation of what their journey means."[21] Either the minister must temper her expectations to match those of the congregation, or she is likely to be ousted.

Peers and Clients

This is in part because ministers, unlike other professionals, have no central organization or single code of ethics to which they can turn for support.[22] While there will always be disagreements on the "treatment of choice" for unusual medical problems, there is nonetheless tremendous cohesion within the medical community. There is a common language understood by all practitioners, and a basic medical view on the world that uses common categories of analysis and interpretation. There is also a strong central organization to provide support for the individual practitioner. And there is a code of ethics that practitioners can use to get support for their decisions.

The same is simply not true in parish ministry.[23] There is no strong central organization and no universally agreed upon ministerial view. Even the language and paradigms used to

143

interpret situations will vary considerably from denomination to denomination and professional to professional. Some will stress sin and judgment; others grace and reconciliation; still others will not use traditional theological language at all, but will talk about brokenness and healing, adopting the language of medicine, humanism, or secular psychology. Clergy are isolated in their practice.[24] They often practice alone, without colleagues to supervise their work or serve as mentors or confidants for their troubles.[25] The significance of lack of a professional organization is summed up by Gerald Jud as follows: "They have no strong central body which sets standards, gives them comfort, and protects them against unfair labor practices."[26]

In their study of ministers who left the parish, Jud et al. point to the problem of lack of peer organization and support as being crucial to some cases of dissatisfaction.[27] Without a professional organization, the role-set (members of the church and community) has tremendous power to determine the proper exercise of the role. While the minister enters the parish with a sense of self as a professional, the autonomy that normally accompanies professional status is severely undermined by the structures of the church. "It appears to him that in order to be successful in his career in the church, he must do the job the organizational way and not the professional way."[28] The problem is exacerbated for women. Patricia Park describes the "erosion of my feelings of authority" that accompanied the rejection of her as a legitimate professional.[29]

Coupled with this lack of professional peer support is another structural difference between clergy and most other professions. While most professionals deal with clients one at a time, clergy deal with an *organized* clientele. A lawyer's clients usually do not know each other; they cannot organize to protect themselves against her practices. Even patients in a hospital, who may know each other by name, deal with professional care-givers on a one-by-one basis. But parishioners are organized: they have church councils, boards of trustees, pastor-parish relations committees, and other structures through which they organize and through which they can, if necessary, organize against the minister. Indeed, informal power structures, such as the women's fellowship, can also wield considerable power.[30] In Ruth's case, for example, if she errs in her handling of Kathy's dilemma and that error comes to the attention of the church, they can present a united front in their efforts to have her ousted. Thus, she has considerably less power to determine how she should function in her job than some sociological analyses would lead one to believe! Some autonomous professionals lack peer support and can be very much at the mercy of their clientele. Some parishioners (e.g., Kathy) will see their minister on a one-to-one basis, but many see the minister only in groups and in her or his public performances.

And this raises yet another issue of structure that affects the power and authority of ministers. Unlike most other professionals, ministers practice in the public eye.[31] Many of their functions are performed before groups, not with individual clients. They lead worship before congregations, conduct meetings of members, and generally work more with groups than with individuals. This means that their work is not as secretive as is the case for other professions.

Moreover, clergy often *live* in the public eye. The practice of having a parsonage—usually right next to the church—means that the minister's private life as well as professional life is open to scrutiny.[32] The minister's home becomes an adjunct to the church, and her or his family is subject to severe role expectations as well. As Marilyn Brown Oden puts it, "What doctor's wife represents the hospital, or lawyer's wife represents the courts, as a minister's wife represents the church?"[33] Not only are ministers always on the job, but so are their families.

And not only do ministers live in the public eye, but their lives and their work are intertwined as no other professional's. What lawyer's divorce would jeopardize his career? What engineer hesitates to take even one beer for fear of what his clients will think? What doctor would be judged a bad doctor because he swore at a nurse? Yet the minister's life-style and personal story can become grounds for negative judgments about her or his professional self. Thus where Bayles argues that "public opinion of a particular professional . . . is of little importance" in the professions, this is clearly not true for ministry.[34]

Combined, these structural realities do much to engender "anomie," or role confusion, and loss of authority on the part of the minister. As Letty Russell puts it, "There are many structural aspects of the system that lead to a breakdown of partnership."[35] Some have argued that a strong professional organization would help to recapture professional power for ministers.[36] Others see little hope except for ministers to add on a second profession such as counseling, with its more traditional authority structures.[37] Lacking structural protections against the vagaries of congregational whims, ministers are extremely vulnerable both emotionally and in terms of their livelihood.[38] They are so far from fitting the traditional image of the "powerful professional" practicing in autonomous authority that, as we have seen, there has been a large debate about whether ministry can even be called a profession.[39]

The Paradox of Power and the "Suffering Servant"

This creates what I call a paradox of power. As a professional, the minister is still powerful and is expected to exercise authority. Particularly in confrontation with individual clients, such as Kathy, ministers have the power to define reality, create expectations, and significantly affect the meaning of people's lives. Yet at the same time, their power is undercut by the structures in which they work. They are both powerful and not powerful. They have authority (legitimated power), but often lack structures that permit its exercise (power to accomplish things).

All professional power is to some extent paradoxical. It is given in order that it be used to serve others. Professional power is meant to be a power *for* rather than a power *over*. It is legitimated only when it is used for the good of another, or of society. Thus, all professionals experience a paradox related to their power: without power, they are not professionals, yet with it they are always in danger of failing to serve and thus being seen as unprofessional. Power is necessary to a professional, and yet it threatens to undermine the very thing it is meant to secure—the authority of the trustee.

This is partly why professional codes stress the "servant" aspect of being a professional. The image of "suffering servant" is a strong one in ministry, and in other professions (medicine, nursing) as well. This image fits well the notion of trusteeship—the trustee serves the other's interests, if necessary at her own expense. Even contemporary feminists who are leery of the traditional "servant" expectations attached to women nonetheless use the image of servant as a model for ministry.[40]

However, the suffering servant image creates some problems for the resolution of professional ethical dilemmas.

This image suggests that problems of professional power can be resolved on an individual level. It directs attention away from the *structures* of professional work, and toward the attitudes and virtues of the practitioner. The image of suffering servant, like the stress on trustworthiness of the practitioner, implies that problems arising in professional practice have to do with the motivations of the professional. Is the professional serving, or is she trying to aggrandize herself? At any point where the professional finds herself lacking adequate power or unable to do what needs to be done, the image of servant suggests that the problem must be a lack of adequate "service" orientation.[41] The ATS study noted that in the face of structural problems in ministry, many ministers lost their sense of the meaningfulness of their work, but thought that "if they were more dedicated, if they possessed greater faith, . . . the sense of meaning and accomplishment would return."[42] This is the kind of response that the suffering servant image invites. Problems are seen as personal problems of motivation and skill.

It is certainly legitimate to ask whether the trustee is truly serving the interests held in trust. And selfishness is certainly a problem in the professions as elsewhere in human life. But exclusive attention to motivation or individual virtue ignores two crucial aspects of the exercise of power. First, it ignores the fact that the professional is not *merely* serving, but is creating reality at the same time. Thus it ignores the reality of the power of definition, which is central to professional power. Thus, on the one hand, it ignores professional power.

Second, it ignores structural limitations on the professional's work. By stressing the autonomy of professional work, sociologists and others have sometimes given the impression that professionals act in total freedom. This is not so. Structures can support and augment professional autonomy and power. But they can also undermine both the image of the professional and the freedom of the professional to choose a particular course of action. Hence, an individualized response that does not account for the importance of structures is simply not adequate. As a result, on the other hand, the suffering servant image ignores the paradox of professional powerlessness.

Ethical Implications

But what does all of this mean for the individual decision-maker? How should it affect the choices made by Ruth? How does an understanding of the limits imposed by structures help a professional facing an ethical dilemma?

First, it helps to understand what the options are. All ethical decisions are made within the context of certain options. "Ought" implies "can"—there can be no obligation to do something that is not possible to do. Understanding the structural realities and limits helps to determine what the options are.

For example, an associate minister once had good reason to think that the senior minister on the staff was working himself so hard as to become physically sick. Yet he refused to slow down or take care of himself. Finally, his illness began to interfere with his work. Not knowing that he was ill, members of the congregation began to complain. The associate minister wanted to inform his denominational body so that his professional colleagues could call him into account and give him some support for slowing down and not trying to be a superman. Given the specific denominational polity, however, any complaints about ministerial performance had to come from the church board. Thus, in order to alert denominational executives to the possible crisis brewing, the associate would first have had to divulge her concerns to members of the church board. This would mean sharing publicly some things that she had learned confidentially and which were not generally known. And this she was reluctant to do.[43]

This associate minister was stalemated because of the denominational structures in which she worked. There was no way for her to seek the advice and monitoring that she believed necessary without violating confidentiality and possibly splitting the church community. Since her concern originated out of care for the cohesion of the community, it would be contradictory for her to take an action that threatened that cohesion. Her options were limited.

Part of discernment, then, is understanding structures and their meaning in our lives. In some cases, we have to accept the limits imposed by the structures. In others, we cannot tackle the immediate problem directly, but have to tackle the structures instead.

Particularly important is understanding how the structures affect the balance of power and what happens to the client in that balance. Since power is central to the professional's position, an examination of the structures of power within the setting is very important. We saw in chapter 1 that moral decision making has to do with locating morally relevant factors in a situation. I argued in chapter 7 that the authority of the professional is such a factor. Professionals have a particular form of power—the power of definition. Accurate discernment of morally relevant factors will involve examining the operation of this power in the situation.

In Ruth's situation, for example, she has considerable power over Kathy. Kathy is an adolescent; she feels alone;

she is scared. All of these factors serve to diminish her self-determination and to heighten the power held by the professional in the situation. The language that Ruth uses as she talks with Kathy can increase or reduce Kathy's fear and aloneness. So can structural aspects of their encounter.

At the same time, professionals experiencing a paradox of power, in which they are simultaneously powerful and powerless, may be inclined to do things that enhance their own power.[44] Not until we see clearly the meaning of structures do we also see clearly our own motivations. Often when we think we are trying to help, we are really trying to take control. A focus on the importance of power and its distribution through the structures in which we act will help us to perceive more clearly what we are really doing.

Discernment Revisited

Such a focus brings us back to the question of the proper description of our acts. Traditional professional ethics has ignored questions of power. When asked to describe what the professional is doing, therefore, the answer would tend to be phrased in paternalistic terms: *helping, healing, solving the problem, giving advice.* All of these answers are partly correct—but only partly. The professional is helping or healing or giving advice or solving problems *within a framework* supported by the profession and limited by societal structures. That framework both gives power to the professional and limits that power. True discernment requires that we pay attention to these matters of power.

This suggests that we may have to revise our understanding of ethical decision making once more. In part I, we saw the importance of prima facie duties and the need to discern morally relevant factors. In part II, we saw that considerations of virtue and character suggest that *some* of those factors are more important than others—namely, those having to do with trust and fidelity. Now in part III, we have added another concern: the crucial factors will also be those that have to do with the balance of power. Questions affecting *justice* emerge

150

as central. And we have added a new norm or duty: liberation. It is only when all these factors are taken into account that we have a sufficient framework for making ethical decisions.

We turn now to see how these factors fit together into a framework for ethical decision making in the professional setting and how that framework might apply to the question of confidentiality in the case of Kathy and Ruth.

CONCLUSION:
CROQUET AND
CONFIDENTIALITY

WE have now come full circle, and it is time to see how our croquet game is to be played. Does the framework developed here help resolve Ruth's ethical dilemma? Should Ruth tell anyone about Kathy's pregnancy and needs, or should she keep confidence?

The Framework

The framework developed here consists of integrating three parts. Since Ruth is faced with a concrete dilemma about what to *do*, we began with questions about right action. Ruth's decision can be neither simply following a rule nor just a matter of calculating consequences. She must balance a set of prima facie duties and discern which of these are most compelling and what it means to act on them in the situation.

Part of the situation is her professional role as minister. While she is bound to the same prima facie duties as everyone else, she also has role expectations. Not all of these are obligatory. However, the aims and images of the profession suggest that she has some role-activated duties.

But when we turn to look at role expectations, we find that expectations for ministers in particular and for professionals in general point toward issues of *character*, not just action. As trustees, all professionals are expected to exhibit the virtue of trustworthiness. Because of the specifics of the Christian story, this virtue is particularly crucial for ministers. Hence, aspects of the situation that have to do with fidelity and trust will be crucial to Ruth's decision. Another important virtue is prudence—accurate discernment of what is going on and willingness to act truthfully.

Accurate discernment requires attention to *structures* and how they influence an ethical dilemma. Attending to the structures of professional practice suggests that professionals have considerable power—the power of definition. Ruth will provide a context of interpretation for the dilemma brought to her by Kathy. She must recognize the power she has as a professional in the situation.

Recognizing the role of professional power also means that aspects of the situation dealing with the balance of power and the oppression of the client will be crucial. In contrast to the traditional view of professional ethics that stresses the norm of beneficence, this framework suggests that several other norms are central. To be trustworthy Ruth must act on norms of justice and liberation that attend her position as a professional.

Of course, she is also bound by the structures of her professional setting. Not everything that she would like to do may be possible for her. These structures affect the balance of power and hence the possibilities for justice and liberation.

This three-part analysis of professional ethics suggests that an adequate ethical framework requires (1) defining and interpreting the situation with a view to discerning morally relevant features that activate general prima facie duties or specific duties of the professional role; (2) living a story that exhibits crucial virtues of trustworthiness and prudence, asking not just, What should I do? but, What kind of person does this?; and (3) attending to structures with a view to issues of power, justice, and liberation.

A Prima Facie Case for Confidentiality

We saw in chapter 8 that Ruth might begin with the question, How will liberation happen here? This forces her to ask where oppression is happening and what liberation would mean in this situation.

Ruth must take cognizance of the general oppression of women in our society and the impact of this oppression on Kathy. Hence, the fact that her client is a woman becomes morally relevant: it means that the client begins in a situation of oppression and general powerlessness. There is not space here to rehearse the various aspects of the oppression of women in our society.[1] But this oppression often centers in women's sexuality. Hence, Kathy's pregnancy and desire for abortion may be a sign of her general oppression.[2]

This does not mean that abortion is automatically the liberating response. It is tempting to think so: Kathy appears to be trapped by her physiology and to need liberation from the limits it sets on her. And certainly securing access to abortion has been a liberating move in general for women in this country.[3]

Yet Ruth must avoid jumping to oversimplified conclusions. I propose that liberation requires two acts on Kathy's part. Ruth's task is to open up the space for Kathy to claim those acts.

First, to be liberated, Kathy must take responsibility for herself and her actions. She must neither participate in patterns of manipulation nor adopt a deceptive view of herself as a victim alone.[4] She must acknowledge her responsibility for the pregnancy and her responsibility for the decision about how to respond to the pregnancy. If Kathy is manipulating or not taking responsibility, Ruth may need to use the confrontive style that reflects the language of liberation.[5]

Second, to be liberated, Kathy must choose an action that permits her to maintain a true story—one that is not destructive or deceptive.[6] Her decision must yield greater, not lesser, integrity for her. It must be coherent with her life story to date, and yet it must not simply be consistent with patterns of oppression represented in that story.

Part of Ruth's task, therefore, is defining the meaning of pregnancy and abortion in the light of the Christian story and in the light of Kathy's own story.[7] However, our focus is not on abortion but on confidentiality. How does keeping or breaking confidence cohere with norms of justice and

154

liberation, and with the prudence and fidelity required of the professional?

A structural limitation is important here. If Kathy is two or more months pregnant, then time is of the essence, for the health risks of abortion increase significantly between the first and second trimesters. Thus, while many ministers responding to the case would have liked time to convince Kathy to share her plight, this time may not be available to Ruth. She must act either to break confidence or to keep confidence now. What should she do?

In discussing a similar case, Bok argues that two of the four premises that normally mandate secrecy do not necessarily mandate it in such an instance.[8] The autonomy of an adolescent is questionable and hence the duty to respect her right to have secrets is diminished. Similarly, where respect for secrets as important to relationships generally mandates keeping confidence, it may not here. Thus, while Bok does not explicitly support the breaking of confidence, she does suggest that the norms of professional behavior that generally support confidentiality may not hold in cases involving pregnant adolescents.

I think that taking justice and liberation seriously yields a different view. Once the power of the professional is understood, being trustworthy takes on new meaning: it requires seeking a balance of power in which justice emerges. Where a client is vulnerable and lacking power, justice requires that power be shared. Minimally, Kathy's oppression and powerlessness should not be increased.

Given the concern for fidelity and justice that must accompany the professional's role, I think two features of this situation are most important: Kathy is alone, and she is feeling powerless.

Because of these two features, I would argue that Ruth should keep confidence. If Kathy is telling the truth, then Ruth is the only person (at least, the only one in authority) she has told about her plight. She is cut off from her "significant others"—her parents do not know, and she is scared of their reaction; her boyfriend (who may provide a haven from her

155

parents in other circumstances) also does not know. It would, of course, be important to find out whether anyone else knows (friends, a family physician). But if Kathy is indeed as alone as she seems, and as vulnerable and powerless as that would make her, then Ruth must be concerned about not increasing Kathy's vulnerability and lack of power.

Since knowledge of a secret gives power,[9] Ruth should begin with a strong bias against divulging Kathy's confidence. Minimally, she should not divulge the information where doing so would simply enhance the power of others over Kathy. Moreover, there is good reason to think that no one should be told. Kathy has chosen to place trust in Ruth. To violate that trust might be to plunge Kathy into a state of utter aloneness, to heighten her vulnerability. This is contrary to the duty of the professional to empower the client, not to increase the client's vulnerability.

In short, a primary concern for justice and liberation, coupled with attention to the structures that give professionals power, suggests that Ruth should *not* break confidence.

Now, we saw in chapter 1 that Ruth could also invoke ancient and strong tradition to support a decision to keep confidence. Both the "seal" and the "privilege" reflect the strong expectation that a minister should keep confidence. Indeed, the term *confidence* means "with fidelity." To be faithful is not to divulge what is told in secret. It seems, then, that both the specific rules of professional ethics and the morally relevant factors brought about by attending to the meaning of trustworthiness in a professional setting give Ruth strong prima facie reasons not to break confidence.

Duties to Others

Yet we also saw above that a strong prima facie case in one direction is not alone sufficient to tell us that Ruth does the right thing if she decides not to share Kathy's information with anyone. There are some good reasons here why she might want to divulge what she has learned. She is concerned about Kathy's good, the parents' rights and interests, the boyfriend's rights and responsibilities, her own collegial obligations, her obligations to the congregation as a whole, and the life of the fetus. All of these factors provide possible extenuating circumstances that might challenge the choice to maintain confidence. Do any of these other considerations activate prima facie duties strong enough to override the weight given to confidentiality by the concerns for justice, trustworthiness, and professional duty?

I think not. But it is important to review briefly some possible arguments for breaking confidence in this case. Others might argue for a different course of action based on a different perception of what is at stake in the situation and how the factors should be weighed. There may be no single right answer to Ruth's difficult dilemma. The strength of different proposals depends on the cogency of the arguments that can be brought to bear.

Perhaps the most cogent arguments are those having to do with Kathy's parents and her boyfriend. Each is implicated in some ways by Kathy's decision. All are owed general duties of respect and justice, such that their desires should be taken into account and they should be given information about things that significantly impact on their lives. And, indeed, one could argue that if Ruth is also their minister, then she has not only these general duties toward them, but some particular, role-activated duties as well.[10]

Moreover, there are theological reasons that would incline Ruth to involve them in the decision. The commandment "Honor thy father and thy mother" reflects the structural importance of family ties and lineages.[11] The notion of covenant, the image of the "body of Christ"—many theological themes could be found that would suggest that Kathy's surrounding community, and particularly her family, should be part of the decision.

When presenting this case, I have found that ministers often respond, "Well, it depends on who the parents are. If I knew them well, and knew that they would really support Kathy, I might tell them." It *does* depend on who the parents are—and how well the minister knows them. But I want to add a cautioning note. In my experience, a high percentage of young people entering ministry have very positive feelings about their own parents. Their father or mother is often one of their significant models or ideal images. This means that ministers are likely to be overly confident about parental love. Ruth should not automatically accept Kathy's negative assessment of her parents' reaction. But Ruth must also be careful lest she read into the situation positive feelings about her own parents *or* value judgments about how parents *should* be. Kathy's parents might indeed kill Kathy—if not literally, perhaps through an indirect retribution for the "disgrace" to their family. Indeed, they may already have killed Kathy symbolically within the family unit, and her pregnancy may be a feeble attempt to assert her separateness and her self. Ruth must be sure that there are adequate checks and balances on her own perceptions. Prayer and honest listening to the definition offered by the client, even if the professional disagrees with it, are necessary for prudence.

Yet we are still left with the question whether Ruth has obligations to the parents (or others) strong enough to override the prima facie case for keeping confidence. I think not. While it is true that Ruth has role-specific duties toward all members of the congregation (including Kathy's parents), she takes on a special obligation when she enters a confidential counseling relationship with Kathy. Part of what it means to be a professional is precisely to be permitted special obligations that allow one's loyalties to be specific to some individuals.[12] While professionals work for the public good, they do so by working for the good of clients and having a primary loyalty to clients. Even those ministers who said it depends on who the parents are were acting out of primary concern for Kathy's well-being, not out of concern for the rights of parents. Thus, Ruth has special obligations to Kathy and it takes a very serious value to override those special obligations.

But could family reconciliation be such a value? Is it strong enough to override the demands of liberation and justice that require above all a refusal to enhance the vulnerability of the client? Reconciliation is certainly a goal that would be affirmed for any minister; indeed, it is sometimes taken to be the overriding goal of ministry.[13] Yet the positive goal of reconciliation is not sufficient to override those special obligations that require explicit loyalty to Kathy. The professional's *primary* duty is liberation of the client. Reconciliation is a goal, but liberation is a duty. And liberation is not the same as reconciliation.

What Ruth must balance is the goal of reconciliation on the one hand versus the demands of trustworthiness and justice on the other. If the purpose of telling Kathy's parents is to create a supportive community for Kathy, Ruth must be careful that the very act of doing so does not undermine those purposes by making Kathy feel even more unsupported and alone. For this reason, most ministers argued that they would not tell the parents without Kathy's consent, though they would try very hard to secure her consent.

Much the same could be said for the other communities suggested above: the boyfriend, the church at large, Kathy's friends. Any of these *might* provide a supportive community for Kathy as she goes through her difficult time of decision. Hence, it is tempting to think that they should be involved. However, if the price of involving them is violation of trust—betrayal—or of the demands of justice and liberation, the price is too high and is not something that the professional can do and still consider herself to be a trustworthy trustee.

Sharing with Peers

The case of Ruth's senior colleague is somewhat different. Traditionally, professionals have assumed that they can share information about clients with one another.[14] And such sharing has been assumed to be covered under the mantle of confidentiality. Indeed, sharing among professional colleagues is so common that some would be surprised to think that it could be defined as a violation of confidence.

Traditionally, sharing among colleagues serves two purposes: it checks perspective or provides advice when needed, and it builds collegiality. Important though I think collegial relationships are, I would urge great caution for Ruth in sharing this information with the senior minister. To do so is to bring into the decision another professional—another person with power. This is contrary to the duty to empower the client and should be done only if Ruth genuinely needs peer counsel and cannot secure it from another professional more distant from the situation. If she does need to share, confidentiality should be discussed and, if possible, the case should be presented so that anonymity is preserved as much as possible—e.g., by presenting the case without using any names. In short, Ruth should pay attention to the ways in which the structures of collegial relationships can be used to distribute power.

However, if Ruth's colleague is also her supervisor, he may be ultimately responsible for anything she does. In this case, given the seriousness of Kathy's situation, Ruth should tell him. Abortion is a volatile moral issue in the Christian community and anyone who bears ultimate responsibility for the spiritual well-being of an adolescent and her family in such a circumstance has a right to be informed. Here, Ruth must pay attention to the structures of her work setting that limit her own authority and give responsibility to a colleague. She must respect the autonomy and need for truth of those who must make decisions or live with the consequences.

Yet even here, this is only a prima facie duty and there are circumstances that would override it. If the supervisor is known not to be trustworthy, if he has a history of not keeping confidence, or if Ruth knows that his own feelings about abortion are so strong that he would do almost anything to try to block a decision for abortion—including threatening Kathy or labeling her a "sinner"—then Ruth must balance her duty to her colleague and supervisor with her duties of fidelity and liberation to the client. Given the nature of professional power, I would argue that the duties of fidelity and liberation are stronger and that Ruth should honor those duties at the expense of duties to her colleague.

This is a striking suggestion to many professionals. As William May notes, many professionals have a strong sense of indebtedness to their colleagues and teachers in the field.[15] Duties toward clients are often seen in "code" terms—more impersonal, distant, and general. Duties toward colleagues, on the other hand, often feel like "covenants"—personal, intimate, and concrete. Thus, if anything, professionals are likely to feel *more* indebted to colleagues than to clients, and to favor their collegial relations even at the expense of clients. The Cornwall Collective notes how hard it is for women to keep the secrets of other women when they work with male colleagues who expect friendship, trust, and openness.[16]

Nonetheless, a careful understanding of the role of professional power should urge caution in sharing information about clients with other professionals. There is a legitimate place for it, to be sure—it provides some protection against distortions of perception and interpretation. But it must also be remembered that most professionals *share* some perceptions and interpretations, and that the weight of joint professional opinion brought against the lone client can be heavy indeed. If we are to take seriously the need for justice and for a redress of the power balance, we must beware of the piling up of professional opinions against the solitary client.

The Duty to Divulge

Classical theological arguments about keeping secrets permit several instances in which even the professional may—or indeed, should—break confidence. One of these is where there is direct threat to another person.

Such reasoning has recently been carried into the law. In a famous case that rocked the professional world, a psychologist with the University of California student health services failed to warn Tatiana Tarasoff that her former lover had indicated an intent to kill her.[17] Tatiana was murdered; her parents sued the university; and the California Supreme Court held that a therapist should break confidence in order to warn a third party of serious danger. Thus, it seems that even confidences received under traditionally protected professional circumstances must be revealed where there is direct threat to someone else.

Is there an analogous situation here? Kathy is contemplating abortion. Should Ruth then break confidence in order to protect the life of the fetus? I think not, though I recognize how difficult and volatile the question of fetal status is today. But there are morally relevant differences between Kathy's situation and the Tarasoff case. Under current law, Kathy has a legal right to abortion.[18] Her contemplated act is not illegal, as was the murder of Tatiana Tarasoff. Since Kathy cannot legally be prevented from securing an abortion, breaking confidence will not necessarily result in protecting the life of the fetus. Nor is there any way to warn the fetus directly. Given all of these factors, the case seems to me significantly different from the Tarasoff case, and I would argue that Ruth has no duty to divulge.

"What If . . ."

But what if Kathy were only twelve? What if the church has taken a public stand against abortion? What if Kathy's father has hit her before? Would changes in any of these factors make a difference—and if so, why? Getting a sense for the factors that matter—factors that, if changed, would change our ethical intuitions—helps us to locate the reasoning process that lies behind justifying an action. I have argued for the moral relevance of some factors that are not always considered in professional ethics—the power of professionals, the reality of oppression, the importance of the story that turns breach of confidentiality into betrayal. But these are not the only factors that might be morally relevant and might influence the decision about what to do.

One such factor is clearly Kathy's age, for this is related to her vulnerability. Suppose Kathy were twenty-seven instead of fifteen. Surely, then, we would not think her quite so vulnerable, nor should she be so lacking in resources. The *meaning* of a pregnancy at age twenty-seven is likely to differ from its meaning at fifteen—and this would need to be examined. Or suppose she were only twelve. The prudent minister needs to see what the pregnancy means and how vulnerable the client is. The duties to share meaning and to empower the client still remain—but they might be acted out differently depending on the particular situation of the client.

Similarly, other factors might make a difference here. The key is to locate the ones that seem to matter, and to press for the *reasons* why they would matter. These reasons can usually be found to relate to factors that touch on basic prima facie duties or role responsibilities. A full argument for what the minister should do will depend on pulling together the reasons, the principles, and the perception of what is happening in the situation. It requires attention to structure, to character, and to the prima facie duties that frame correct action.

What Actually Happened

Since this is a real case, some readers are no doubt wondering what actually did happen. The story is an interesting one.

"Ruth" was not personally or theologically opposed to abortion, nor had her denomination taken an explicit stand against it. Nonetheless, she was concerned about the impact of such a decision on the life of "Kathy." She knew that no matter what Kathy decided, she would live with the decision for the rest of her life. That is a heavy burden for an adolescent. Ruth also felt some responsibility toward Kathy's parents, since her position at the church included some general forms of ministry besides youth work. She therefore decided that, if possible, Kathy should tell at least one of her parents.

In this case, a structural problem actually assisted the resolution of the dilemma. Though Kathy had no money, she could secure an abortion under her parents' medical insurance. But this meant that a record of the procedure might enter Kathy's home through an insurance bill or report. Ruth therefore convinced Kathy that it was too risky not to tell her parents—or at least one of them. Kathy finally agreed to tell her mother.

With Ruth present, Kathy shared her plight with her mother. Her mother supported the decision for an abortion, and gave support in general to Kathy. Together, they decided not to tell Kathy's father, for fear of his temper and possible retribution toward Kathy or her boyfriend.

Kathy did finally have an abortion—with her mother at her side. She thus had at least a small community of support—and an important one. Further, Ruth did not break confidence, since Kathy herself divulged her plight.

It sounds like a story with a happy ending, at least from the perspective of Ruth's professional obligations. In some ways, Ruth did what most ministers hearing the case have suggested would be best: without breaking confidence, she managed to involve the family and provide a supportive community for Kathy.

Yet the story will not end here. Kathy's mother now shares the burden of confidentiality. Does she feel alienated from her husband because she has not shared something so important with him? It is important to remember that anyone with whom confidence is shared then takes on an ethical dilemma. Each must decide whether to keep confidence. Community is gained for one person at the expense of a new dilemma for someone else. Kathy is empowered at the expense of creating some pain and vulnerability for her mother. Ethical issues are rarely single decisions affecting only one or two people.

Moreover, Kathy's life story now includes an abortion. She must reconcile that with her Christian faith. So Ruth's professional obligations are ongoing. This is not wrong; it is the stuff of human life. But it does suggest that we need an ethical framework that accounts for continuity of action. Both Ruth and Kathy will need to think about the stories they are living and the characters they are forming as they make ethical decisions.

In the real world, we rarely live "happily ever after." Perhaps, as Hauerwas suggests, the crux is to have a story—and an ethical system—strong enough to deal with the truth of human life.[19]

NOTES

Introduction: The Croquet Game

1. The recent "Readiness for Ministry" study by the Association of Theological Schools indicates that laity rate work with children and youth very high for beginning clergy. See David S. Schuller, Merton P. Strommen, and Milo L. Brekke, eds., *Ministry in America* (San Francisco: Harper & Row, 1980), pp. 78, 99. This may account in part for why so many beginning ministers are given the task of dealing with the youth groups of the church.
2. Cf. Sissela Bok, *Secrets: On the Ethics of Concealment and Revelation* (New York: Pantheon Books, 1982), p. 124.
3. While recognizing that ministry is carried out by laypeople and ordained clergy alike, as well as by other professionals, I will use the terms *minister* and *ministry* in this volume largely to refer to the ordained clergy.
4. The reissue of Nolan B. Harmon's *Ministerial Ethics and Etiquette* (Nashville: Abingdon Press) in 1978 with nary a change from its original 1928 edition indicates the paucity of materials on professional ethics for ministers. Happily, within the last several years, new volumes addressing this concern have emerged. See, for example, Dennis M. Campbell, *Doctors, Lawyers, Ministers: Christian Ethics in Professional Practice* (Nashville: Abingdon Press, 1982).
5. Samuel Gorovitz and Bruce Miller, *Professional Responsibility in the Law (A Curriculum Report from the Institute on Law and Ethics, Summer 1977)* (The Council for Philosophical Studies, 1977).
6. See, for example, Stanley Hauerwas, *Vision and Virtue: Essays in Christian Ethical Reflection* (Notre Dame, Ind.: Fides Publishers, 1974); and *Truthfulness and Tragedy: Further Investigations into Christian Ethics* (Notre Dame, Ind.: University of Notre Dame Press, 1977); and James William McClendon, Jr., *Biography as Theology* (Nashville: Abingdon Press, 1974). Approaches to ethics that focus on structures include most contemporary liberation theologies.
7. See, for instance, Lisa H. Newton, "A Professional Ethic: A Proposal in Context," in John E. Thomas, ed., *Matters of Life and Death* (Toronto: Samuel Stevens, 1978).
8. Cf. Peter Jarvis, "The Ministry: Occupation, Profession or Status?" in *The Expository Times* 86, no. 9 (June 1975): 264-67; Thomas M. Gannon, S.J.,

"Priest/Minister: Profession or Non-Profession?" in *Review of Religious Research* 12, no. 2 (Winter 1971); James D. Glasse, *Profession: Minister* (Nashville: Abingdon Press, 1968); Dudley Strain, *The Measure of a Minister* (St. Louis, Mo.: The Bethany Press, 1964).

9. Lewis Carroll, *Alice in Wonderland* in Martin Gardner, *The Annotated Alice* (New York: Bramhall House, 1960), pp. 111-12.

10. Ibid., p. 113.

1. Rules and Situations

1. Bernard Mayo, "Ethics of Virtue Versus Ethics of Principle," in William K. Frankena and John T. Granrose, eds., *Introductory Readings in Ethics* (Englewood Cliffs, N.J.: Prentice-Hall, 1974), p. 233.

2. The identical statement appears both in the Congregational code and in the Methodist ministers' ethical code. See Harmon, *Ministerial Ethics and Etiquette,* pp. 201, 204.

3. Bok, *Secrets,* p. 78.

4. Cf. Robert E. Regan, *Professional Secrecy in the Light of Moral Principles* (Washington, D.C.: Augustinian Press, 1943) and Thomas Joseph O'Donnell, *Morals in Medicine* (Westminster, Md.: Newman Press, 1960), esp. chap. 7.

5. Roy D. Weinberg, *Confidential and Other Privileged Communication* (Dobbs Ferry, N.Y.: Oceana Publications, 1967), see esp. chap. 5. See also Lindell L. Gumper, *Legal Issues in the Practice of Ministry* (Birmingham, Mich.: Psychological Studies and Consultation Program, 1981).

6. Robert L. Stoyles, "The Dilemma of the Constitutionality of the Priest-Penitent Privilege—The Application of the Religion Clauses," *University of Pittsburgh Law Review* 29 (1967): 27-63.

7. Weinberg, *Confidential and Other Privileged Communication,* p. 2: "The most commonly advanced argument in support of privilege is that it encourages vital interpersonal relationships which might be seriously prejudiced by the prospect of breached confidentiality."

8. See the discussions of rule-utilitarianism in Michael D. Bayles, *Contemporary Utilitarianism* (New York: Doubleday, 1968).

9. Adrienne Rich, *On Lies, Secrets and Silence* (New York: W. W. Norton, 1979), p. 192.

10. Bok, *Secrets,* p. 85.

11. Cf. John Stuart Mill, *Utilitarianism* (New York: The Bobbs-Merrill Co., 1957).

12. Bok argues that "the premises of autonomy and of relationship do not necessarily mandate secrecy" in circumstances where a professional is dealing with a young adolescent. *Secrets,* p. 125.

13. Ibid.

14. Michael D. Bayles, *Professional Ethics* (Belmont, Calif.: Wadsworth, 1981), p. 92.

15. As Harmon suggests, codes of ministerial ethics often focus on "the attempt to clarify the relationship between members of the profession." *Ministerial Ethics and Etiquette,* p. 71.

16. Cf. Letty M. Russell, *The Future of Partnership* (Philadelphia: The Westminster Press, 1979), p. 106.

17. John T. Noonan, Jr., "An Almost Absolute Value in History" in *The Morality of Abortion: Legal and Historical Perspectives* (Cambridge, Mass.: Harvard University Press, 1970).
18. Joseph Fletcher, *Situation Ethics* (Philadelphia: The Westminster Press, 1966); and *Moral Responsibility: Situation Ethics at Work* (Philadelphia: The Westminster Press, 1967); see also Harvey Cox, ed., *The Situation Ethics Debate* (Philadelphia: The Westminster Press, 1968).
19. For a discussion of the residue of remorse or regret left by our sense of obligations, see James F. Childress, "Just-War Criteria" in Thomas A. Shannon, ed., *War or Peace?: The Search for New Answers* (Maryknoll, N.Y.: Orbis Books, 1980).
20. Arthur J. Dyck, *On Human Care: An Introduction to Ethics* (Nashville: Abingdon Press, 1977), see chap. 5.
21. Cf. G. J. Warnock, *The Object of Morality* (London: Methuen & Co., 1971), chap. 3.
22. James M. Gustafson, "Context Versus Principles: A Misplaced Debate in Christian Ethics," in *Christian Ethics and the Community* (Philadelphia: Pilgrim Press, 1971).
23. Exception to the requirement for confidentiality has been maintained in circumstances where another person is endangered. Cf. O'Donnell, *Morals in Medicine,* p. 327; California Supreme Court, *Tarasoff v. Regents of the University of California* (131 California Reporter 14, 1976); and Bok, *Secrets,* chap. 9.
24. Hauerwas, *Vision and Virtue,* chap. 1.
25. W. D. Ross, *The Right and the Good* (Oxford: Clarendon Press, 1930), chap. 2.
26. Cf. the method proposed by Philip Wogaman in *A Christian Method of Moral Judgment* (Philadelphia: The Westminster Press, 1976).
27. One need not be an intuitionist in order to make use of the concept of prima facie duties; see, for example, Childress, "Just-War Criteria."
28. William K. Frankena, "The Concept of Social Justice," in Richard B. Brandt, ed., *Social Justice* (Englewood Cliffs, N.J.: Prentice-Hall, 1962).
29. Tom L. Beauchamp and James F. Childress, *Principles of Biomedical Ethics,* 2d ed. (New York: Oxford University Press, 1983), pp. 191-97.
30. James M. Gustafson, "Moral Discernment in the Christian Life" in *Theology and Christian Ethics* (Philadelphia: Pilgrim Press, 1974).
31. Ibid., p. 104.
32. Ibid.
33. This observation was first made by the Reverend Jacqueline Meadows from Sacramento, California. Subsequently, other clergy have also noted the similarity between Kathy's description of her own parents and her decision about what to do.

2. Roles and Morality

1. Robert M. Veatch, "Medical Ethics: Professional or Universal," *Harvard Theological Review* 65, no. 4 (October 1972): 531.
2. William C. Starr, "Professions and Advertising," *Business and Professional Ethics* 2, no. 2 (Winter 1979): 9. As Harmon puts it, "Whether we like it or not, the people demand a higher standard from the

minister than from the ordinary man." *Ministerial Ethics and Etiquette,* p. 22.

3. Cf. Jane Clapp, *Professional Ethics and Insignia* (Metuchen, N.J.: The Scarecrow Press, 1974).

4. For example, as the American Occupational Medical Association strove to distinguish itself from the American Medical Association, it developed a "code of ethical conduct for physicians providing occupational medical services." Cf. *Journal of Occupational Medicine* 18 (August 1976).

5. Beauchamp and Childress, *Principles of Biomedical Ethics,* 2d ed., p. 106.

6. Renee C. Fox, *Experiment Perilous* (Philadelphia: University of Pennsylvania Press, 1959), p. 115. See also Eliot Freidson, *Profession of Medicine: A Study of the Sociology of Applied Knowledge* (New York: Dodd, Mead, 1973), pp. 231-32.

7. Dorothy Emmet, *Rules, Roles and Relations* (New York: Macmillan, 1967), p. 147.

8. Cf. Brita Gill, "A Ministry of Presence," in Judith L. Weidman, ed., *Women Ministers* (San Francisco: Harper & Row, 1981), p. 104: "We must not think of ourselves as simply professionals performing a role."

9. Emmet, *Rules, Roles and Relations,* p. 13.

10. Edwin M. Lemert, "Role Enactment, Self, and Identity in the Systematic Check Forger," in *Human Deviance, Social Problems, and Social Control* (Englewood Cliffs, N.J.: Prentice-Hall, 1967), p. 119.

11. James W. Kennedy, *Ministers' Shop-Talk* (New York: Harper & Row, 1965), p. 178. See also Harmon, *Ministerial Ethics and Etiquette.*

12. Emmet, *Rules, Roles and Relations,* p. 15.

13. Ibid., p. 40.

14. Veatch, "Medical Ethics: Professional or Universal," p. 542.

15. Bayles, *Professional Ethics,* p. 21.

16. Kenneth Kipnis, "Professional Ethics," *Business and Professional Ethics* 2, no. 1 (Fall 1978): 2-3.

17. Bayles concurs with Kipnis. He argues, "As parental roles to care for children create an obligation for parents that other people do not have, so occupying a professional role can entail obligations for professionals that others do not have." *Professional Ethics,* p. 20.

18. Onora O'Neill, "Begetting, Bearing and Rearing," in Onora O'Neill and William Ruddick, eds., *Having Children* (New York: Oxford University Press, 1979), pp. 25-38.

19. Chris Hackler, "Is Medical Ethics Unique?" *Business and Professional Ethics* 2, no. 3/4 (Spring/Summer 1979): 4.

20. Strain, *Measure of a Minister,* p. 70.

21. John B. Coburn, *Minister: Man-in-the-Middle* (New York: Macmillan, 1963), p. 143.

22. Harmon, *Ministerial Ethics and Etiquette,* p. 99.

3. Expectations and Obligations: Roles in Action

1. Ann Douglas, *The Feminization of American Culture* (New York: Avon Books, 1977), see esp. chaps. 1–3. Harmon's *Ministerial Ethics and*

Etiquette, originally published in 1928, represents the culmination of this view of clergy.

2. A second watershed may have happened during the late 1960s and early 1970s. In the ATS "Readiness for Ministry" study, David Schuller argues that the concept of ministry has undergone significant change during the past decade. See Schuller, Strommen, and Brekke, *Ministry in America,* p. 3. The number of books emerging in the late 1960s and early 1970s dealing with issues of conflict in clergy role suggests that it was a particularly turbulent time during which the role underwent significant change. See, for example, Charles Prestwood, *A New Breed of Clergy* (Grand Rapids: Wm. B. Eerdmans Publishing Co., 1972).

3. Bayles argues that the aims of a profession alone are not sufficient to determine obligations, but that obligations depend on the balance of values to be upheld in a liberal society. See Bayles, *Professional Ethics,* p. 19.

4. Newton, "A Professional Ethic," p. 268.

5. In Stanley Joel Reiser, Arthur J. Dyck, and William J. Curran, *Ethics in Medicine: Historical Perspectives and Contemporary Concerns* (Cambridge, Mass.: Massachusetts Institute of Technology, 1977), p. 5.

6. Samuel Southard, *Pastoral Authority in Personal Relationships* (Nashville: Abingdon Press, 1969), p. 138.

7. For example, Letty Russell argues that "in my opinion, ordination should be for the purpose of subverting the 'clergy line' and changing the structures of the church, so that the whole people of God might once again find ways to exercise their spiritual gifts of services." In *Future of Partnership,* p. 134.

8. See, for example, Howard E. Kershner, "What Should the Churches Do About Social Problems?" in Paul T. Gersild and Dale A. Johnson, eds., *Moral Issues and Christian Response* (New York: Holt, Rinehart & Winston, 1976), pp. 36-40; Browne Barr and Mary Eakin, *The Ministering Congregation* (Philadelphia: United Church Press, 1972), p. 42; and an indictment of this position by Blanqui Otano-Rivera, "The Task of Enabling," in Weidman, *Women Ministers,* p. 163.

9. Richard A. McCormick, S.J., "Human Rights and the Mission of the Church," in Gerald H. Anderson and Thomas F. Stransky, C.S.P., eds., *Mission Trends 4* (New York: Paulist Press, 1979): 37-50, at p. 40: "The phrase 'genuinely priestly work'—taken exclusively to mean preaching and administration of the sacraments—must be seen as a relic."

10. Merton P. Strommen flatly declares that "major denominations can be classified on the basis of their concept of the clergy's task." See Merton P. Strommen, "Models of Ministry," in Schuller, Strommen, and Brekke, *Ministry in America,* p. 55. This volume does much to support the notion that there are denominational differences in perspectives on ministry and also helps to define those differences along a spectrum.

11. Gerald J. Jud, et al., *Ex-Pastors: Why Men Leave the Parish Ministry* (Philadelphia: Pilgrim Press, 1970), p. 80.

12. Charles Merrill Smith, *How to Become a Bishop Without Being Religious* (New York: Doubleday, 1965), pp. 10-11. Variations are appropriate to different cultural subgroups or regions, however, and it is possible for a flamboyant minister to be extremely popular and effective.

13. Harmon, *Ministerial Ethics and Etiquette,* p. 193.
14. Strain, *Measure of a Minister,* p. 46.
15. Patricia Park, "Women and Liturgy," in Weidman, *Women Ministers,* p. 81.
16. William E. Hulme, *Your Pastor's Problems: A Guide for Ministers and Laymen* (New York: Doubleday, 1966), pp. 41-42.
17. Strommen, "Models of Ministry," p. 81. See also Hulme, *Your Pastor's Problems,* p. 91.
18. Daniel O. Aleshire, "Eleven Major Areas of Ministry," in Schuller, Strommen, and Brekke, *Ministry in America,* suggests, "The minister or priest as the imitation of Christ is still a basic expectation for some people," p. 37.
19. Joan Didion, *The White Album* (New York: Simon & Schuster, 1979), p. 11.
20. Robert M. Veatch, "Models for Ethical Medicine in Revolutionary Age," *The Hastings Center Report* 2, no. 3 (June 1972): 5-7.
21. Veatch's understanding of the role of "priest" would obviously be challenged by some of those concerned about the aims, images, and models of ministry.
22. Similarly, Bayles offers criticisms of both of these models. See Bayles, *Professional Ethics,* pp. 61-67. For both Veatch and Bayles, a central issue is whether the professional has the authority to impose value judgments on the client. This may be a place where ministry will differ from other professions, and we will return to this issue in part III.
23. Bayles, *Professional Ethics,* p. 68.
24. Russell, *Future of Partnership,* pp. 73-74.
25. David K. Switzer, *Pastor, Preacher, Person: Developing a Pastoral Ministry in Depth* (Nashville: Abingdon Press, 1979), p. 13.
26. Ibid., p. 47.
27. See Harmon, *Ministerial Ethics and Etiquette,* p. 9: "It is accepted as an axiom that every minister is a Christian gentleman."
28. Rich, "Toward a Woman-Centered University," in *On Lies, Secrets and Silence;* The Cornwall Collective, *Your Daughters Shall Prophesy: Feminist Alternatives in Theological Education* (New York: Pilgrim Press, 1980), see esp. chaps. 2 and 3; see also Park, "Women and Liturgy," p. 78.
29. Karl Menninger, *Whatever Became of Sin?* (New York: Hawthorne Books, 1973), pp. 45ff.
30. Wendy Carlton, *"In Our Professional Opinion . . .": The Primacy of Clinical Judgment Over Moral Choice* (Notre Dame, Ind.: University of Notre Dame Press, 1978).
31. Charles L. Bosk, *Forgive and Remember: Managing Medical Failure* (Chicago: The University of Chicago Press, 1979).
32. H. Richard Niebuhr, *The Purpose of the Church and Its Ministry: Reflections on the Aims of Theological Education* (New York: Harper & Brothers, 1956).
33. See Schuller, Strommen, and Brekke, *Ministry in America;* see also Glasse, *Profession: Minister;* and Jud, et al., *Ex-Pastors.*
34. Rockwell C. Smith, et al., *Sociological Studies of an Occupation: The Ministry* (Evanston, Ill.: Garrett-Evangelical Theological Seminary, 1974), see esp. chap. 3.

35. Donald P. Smith, *Clergy in the Cross Fire: Coping with Role Conflict in the Ministry* (Philadelphia: The Westminster Press, 1973).
36. M. Helene Pollock, "Growing Toward Effective Ministry," in Weidman, *Women Ministers*, p. 17.
37. Cf. Emmet, *Rules, Roles and Relations*, at p. 147: "A person finds himself in more than one constellation of roles . . . and also in tensions between different claims within the same 'role-set'."
38. Jud, et al., *Ex-Pastors*, p. 88. See also Coburn's *Minister: Man-in-the-Middle*, pp. 186-87.
39. For example, Virginia Barksdale suggests that church officials expect to see programming and community service that are not always appropriate in a small church. See "Small Church—Big Family," in Weidman, *Women Ministers*, p. 38.
40. Hulme, *Your Pastor's Problems*, p. 41. Lora Gross argues that the result is a separation of the "female" and the "male" parts of ourselves with the net result that "what we have then in both the church and society are subordinate female bodies and dominant disembodied males as a gender system which forms the basis for an entire social system." See "The Embodied Church," in Weidman, *Women Ministers*, p. 40.
41. Donald P. Smith, *Clergy in the Cross Fire.*
42. Robert J. Levine, "Case Study—Medical Students as Social Scientists: Are There Role Conflicts?" *IRB: A Review of Human Subjects Research* 2, no. 1 (January 1980): 6-8.
43. Judith P. Swazey, "Commentary—Role Conflicts of Social Scientists," *IRB: A Review of Human Subjects Research* 2, no. 1 (January 1980): 8.

4. Being Professional

1. Harmon, *Ministerial Ethics and Etiquette*, p. 34.
2. Strain, *Measure of a Minister*, p. 21.
3. Coburn, *Minister: Man-in-the-Middle*, p. 159.
4. Switzer, *Pastor, Preacher, Person*, p. 16.
5. Gill, "Ministry of Presence," p. 91.
6. David S. Schuller, "Identifying the Criteria for Ministry," in Schuller, Strommen, and Brekke, *Ministry in America*, p. 19.
7. Ibid., pp. 19-20.
8. Aleshire, "Eleven Major Areas of Ministry," p. 36.
9. Hulme, *Your Pastor's Problems*, p. 91.
10. James Gustafson, "The Clergy in the United States," in Kenneth S. Lynn, et al., *The Professions in America* (Boston: Beacon Press, 1967), p. 82.
11. Southard, *Pastoral Authority*, p. 45.
12. Owen Brandon, *The Pastor and His Ministry* (London: S.P.C.K., 1972), p. 105.
13. Urban T. Holmes III, *The Future Shape of Ministry* (New York: The Seabury Press, 1971), p. 198.
14. Cf. Bayles, *Professional Ethics*, p. 7; Glasse, *Profession: Minister*, p. 38; Darrell Reeck, *Ethics for the Professions: A Christian Perspective* (Minneapolis: Augsburg Publishing House, 1982), p. 18.
15. Bayles, *Professional Ethics*, p. 8.

16. Freidson, *Profession of Medicine*, p. 71; Dennis M. Campbell, *Doctors, Lawyers, Ministers*, p. 22.
17. Glasse, *Profession: Minister*, p. 38; Dennis M. Campbell, *Doctors, Lawyers, Ministers*, p. 24.
18. Dennis M. Campbell, *Doctors, Lawyers, Ministers*, p. 23.
19. Strain, *Measure of a Minister*, p. 19.
20. Newton, "A Professional Ethic," p. 264.
21. Ibid.
22. June Goodfield, "Reflections on the Hippocratic Oaths," *The Hastings Center Studies* 1, no. 2 (1973): 90.
23. Charles Merrill Smith, *How To Become a Bishop*, p. 1.
24. Ibid., pp. 6-9 passim.
25. Clapp, *Professional Ethics and Insignia*, p. 224.
26. Cf. the Code of the American Dietetic Association in Clapp, *Professional Ethics and Insignia*, pp. 239-40. See also Harmon, *Ministerial Ethics and Etiquette*.
27. For a concurring view, see Albert R. Jonsen, S.J., and Andre E. Hellegers, "Conceptual Foundations for an Ethics of Medical Care," in Laurence R. Tancredi, ed., *Ethics of Health Care* (Washington, D.C.: National Academy of Sciences, 1974), p. 8. In *Principles of Biomedical Ethics* (2d ed.), Beauchamp and Childress argue that "professional codes often stress virtues in addition to duties and ideal actions" (p. 266). My perspective here is a bit different. I am arguing that injunctions in codes that appear to be statements about duties are actually often hidden statements about virtues.
28. A. M. Carr-Saunders and P. A. Wilson, *The Professions* (Oxford: Clarendon Press, 1933).
29. Ibid., p. 421.
30. Carnegie Samuel Calian, *Today's Pastor in Tomorrow's World* (New York: Hawthorne Books, 1977), pp. 104-5.
31. Jud, et al., *Ex-Pastors*, p. 74.
32. Charles Merrill Smith, *How to Become a Bishop*, p. 2.
33. Emmet, *Rules, Roles and Relations*, p. 172.
34. Carr-Saunders and Wilson, *The Professions*.
35. These terms have emerged every year in my course on professional ethics.
36. Newton, "A Professional Ethic."
37. Emmet, *Rules, Roles and Relations*, p. 172.
38. Ibid., p. 162.
39. Edmund D. Pellegrino, *Humanism and the Physician* (Knoxville: University of Tennessee Press, 1979), p. 106.
40. Bayles, *Professional Ethics*, p. 75.
41. Aleshire, "Eleven Major Areas of Ministry," p. 30.
42. Thomas C. Campbell, "United Church of Christ," in Schuller, Strommen, and Brekke, *Ministry in America*, p. 496.
43. Southard, *Pastoral Authority*, p. 83.
44. Coburn, *Minister: Man-in-the-Middle*, p. 131.
45. Indeed, Reeck asserts that "character is basic to all ethics and to professional ethics in particular." *Ethics for the Professions*, p. 42.

46. See the Code of Professional Responsibility of the American Bar Association in Clapp, *Professional Ethics and Insignia,* p. 409.
47. Emmet, *Rules, Roles and Relations,* p. 163.

5. The Trustworthy Trustee

1. Mayo, "Ethics of Virtue Versus Ethics of Principle," p. 233.
2. William K. Frankena, "Prichard and the Ethics of Virtues," in K. E. Goodpaster, ed., *Perspectives on Morality: Essays by William K. Frankena* (Notre Dame, Ind.: University of Notre Dame Press, 1976).
3. Hauerwas, *Truthfulness and Tragedy,* p. 20.
4. Bayles, *Professional Ethics,* pp. 72, 83.
5. Mayo, "Ethics of Virtue Versus Ethics of Principle," p. 234; see also J. O. Urmson, "Saints and Heroes," in Joel Feinberg, ed., *Moral Concepts* (London: Oxford University Press, 1970).
6. William F. May, "Notes on the Ethics of Doctors and Lawyers" (Bloomington, Ind.: Indiana University Press, 1977), p. 4.
7. Paul Ramsey, *Deeds and Rules in Christian Ethics* (New York: Charles Scribner's Sons, 1967), p. 140.
8. Hauerwas, *Vision and Virtue,* chap. 3.
9. Gill, "A Ministry of Presence," p. 96.
10. Bok, *Secrets,* p. 84.
11. Ibid., p. 102.
12. Ibid., p. 121.
13. McClendon, *Biography as Theology,* p. 21.
14. Hauerwas, *Truthfulness and Tragedy,* p. 20, argues that our character is not acquired through the decisions we make but by the convictions that we hold. Here, I disagree a bit, as I believe that the action itself once taken has an objective character that must then be incorporated into our ongoing story.
15. Karen Lebacqz, "Abortion: Getting the Ethics Straight," *Logos* (Spring 1982).
16. Cf. Hauerwas, *Truthfulness and Tragedy,* chap. 5.
17. Carl D. Schneider, *Shame, Exposure and Privacy* (Boston: Beacon Press, 1977), argues that it is primarily our embarrassing moments that we remember and struggle to incorporate into our ongoing life story.
18. Hauerwas, *Vision and Virtue,* chap. 4.
19. Maurice Mandelbaum, *The Phenomenology of Moral Experience* (Baltimore: Johns Hopkins Press, 1969), p. 158.
20. For example, charisma, depth of faith, certainty, and fortitude might be distinctive virtues of clergy.
21. Talcott Parsons, *Essays in Sociological Theology,* rev. ed. (Glencoe, Ill.: The Free Press, 1954), p. 372; cf. also Freidson, *Profession of Medicine,* p. xvii.
22. Freidson, *Profession of Medicine,* p. 71.
23. Morris L. Cogan, "Toward a Definition of Profession," *Harvard Educational Review* 23 (1953): 33-50.
24. Coburn, *Minister: Man-in-the-Middle,* p. 134.
25. Bernard Barber, "Regulation and the Professions," *The Hastings Center Report* 10, no. 1 (February 1980): 34.

26. Ibid.; see also Everett C. Hughes, "Professions," in Lynn, et al., *Professions in America*, pp. 2-3.
27. Dennis M. Campbell, *Doctors, Lawyers, Ministers*, pp. 37-38.
28. Freidson, *Profession of Medicine*, p. xvii.
29. Sissela Bok, *Lying: Moral Choice in Public and Private Life* (New York: Pantheon Books, 1978), p. 85.
30. Holmes, *Future Shape of Ministry*, p. 247; see also Neely Dixon McCarter, *Designing Theological Curriculum* (Neely Dixon McCarter, 1979), p. 20.
31. Strain, *Measure of a Minister*, p. 50.
32. Cf. Rockwell C. Smith et al., *Sociological Studies of an Occupation*, p. 28. Similarly, Harmon argues that "whether we like it or not, the people demand a higher standard from the minister," *Ministerial Ethics and Etiquette*, p. 22; and Hulme quotes a church councilman as saying, "I want my minister to be a cut above *me*," *Your Pastor's Problems*, p. 94.
33. Gill, "Ministry of Presence," p. 98. See also Max Thurian, *Priesthood and Ministry: Ecumenical Research* (London: Mowbray, 1970), p. 13.
34. Paul Ramsey, *The Patient as Person* (New Haven: Yale University Press, 1970), p. xiii; also Dennis M. Campbell, *Doctors, Lawyers, Ministers*, p. 104.
35. Rich, "Women and Honor: Some Notes on Lying," in *On Lies, Secrets and Silence*, p. 192.

6. From Virtue to Vision: The Prudent Professional

1. Mandelbaum, *Phenomenology of Moral Experience*.
2. A. C. Ewing, *Ethics* (New York: The Free Press, 1953), chap. 8.
3. Mayo, "Ethics of Virtue Versus Ethics of Principle," p. 231.
4. Mandelbaum, *Phenomenology of Moral Experience*, p. 153.
5. Arthur J. Dyck, "A Unified Theory of Virtue and Obligation," *Journal of Religious Ethics* 1, no. 1 (1973): 37-52.
6. Cf. Hauerwas, *Vision and Virtue*, chap. 3; and *Truthfulness and Tragedy*, chap. 1.
7. Adolf Guggenbühl-Craig, *Power in the Helping Professions* (Dallas: Spring Publications, 1979).
8. Veatch, "Medical Ethics: Professional or Universal."
9. Cornwall, *Your Daughters Shall Prophesy*, p. 3.
10. Hauerwas, *Vision and Virtue*, p. 80.
11. G. E. M. Anscombe, *Intention* (Ithaca: Cornell University Press, 1957), p. 37.
12. Didion, *White Album*, p. 11.
13. Hauerwas, *Vision and Virtue*, p. 75.
14. Alasdair MacIntyre, *After Virtue* (Notre Dame, Ind.: University of Notre Dame Press, 1981).
15. Hauerwas, *Truthfulness and Tragedy*, p. 21.
16. Ibid., p. 35.
17. E.g., Hauerwas suggests that "a true story must be one that helps me to go on." Ibid., p. 80.
18. Cf. Hauerwas, "Medicine as a Tragic Profession," in *Truthfulness and Tragedy*.

19. Aleshire, "Eleven Major Areas of Ministry," p. 37.
20. Juan Luis Segundo, *The Liberation of Theology* (Maryknoll, N.Y.: Orbis Books, 1979), chap. 4.
21. Cf. Frederick S. Carney, "The Virtue-Obligation Controversy," *Journal of Religious Ethics* 1, no. 1 (1973): 5-19.
22. Brian O. McDermott, S.J., "Power and Parable in Jesus' Ministry," in Thomas E. Clarke, ed., *Above Every Name: The Lordship of Christ and Social Systems* (New York: Paulist Press, 1980), p. 88.
23. Reeck, *Ethics for the Professions*, p. 44.
24. *Webster's New Collegiate Dictionary* (Springfield, Mass.: G. C. Merriam Co., 1974), p. 929.
25. Josef Pieper, *The Four Cardinal Virtues* (Notre Dame, Ind.: University of Notre Dame Press, 1975), p. 4.
26. Dom Helder Camara, *A Thousand Reasons for Living* (Philadelphia: Fortress Press, 1981), p. 111.
27. Pieper, *Four Cardinal Virtues*, p. 6.
28. *Webster's*, p. 929.
29. James M. Gustafson, *Theology and Christian Ethics* (Philadelphia: Pilgrim Press, 1974), p. 118.
30. Pieper, *Four Cardinal Virtues*, p. 13.
31. Hulme, *Your Pastor's Problems*, p. 55.
32. Pieper, *Four Cardinal Virtues*, p. 13.

7. Professional Power

1. Cf. O'Neill, "Begetting, Bearing, and Rearing."
2. Cf. Beauchamp and Childress, *Principles of Biomedical Ethics*, 2d ed., pp. 168ff. Hulme argues that when it comes to time, "the ministry is like parenthood." See *Your Pastor's Problems*, p. 134.
3. Charles Fried, *Right and Wrong* (Cambridge, Mass.: Harvard University Press, 1978), p. 179.
4. Hulme, *Your Pastor's Problems*, p. 42.
5. See Southard, *Pastoral Authority*, p. 61; and Strain, *Measure of a Minister*, p. 16.
6. Russell, *Future of Partnership*, p. 35; cf. John 15:14-15.
7. Switzer argues that the church is the family of God. See *Pastor, Preacher, Person*, pp. 31-32.
8. Indeed, H. Richard Niebuhr argues that the use of the office signals a new paradigm for ministry. See *Purpose of the Church and Its Ministry*, pp. 80-81.
9. Hughes, "Professions," p. 3.
10. McCarter, *Designing Theological Curriculum*, p. 21; and Jud, et al., *Ex-Pastors*, p. 86.
11. Bok, *Secrets*, p. 80.
12. Ibid.
13. Switzer, *Pastor, Preacher, Person*, p. 17.
14. Parsons, *Essays in Sociological Theory*, p. 392; Bernard Lonergan, "Dialectic of Authority," in Frederick J. Adelmann, S.J., *Authority* (The Hague: Martinus Nijhoff, 1974), p. 24.
15. Switzer, *Pastor, Preacher, Person*, p. 18.

177

16. Indeed, as Hughes puts it, "A professional has a license to deviate from lay conduct . . . ; it is an institutionalized deviation." Cf. "Professions," p. 2.
17. Cf. Hulme, *Your Pastor's Problems,* p. 106.
18. Strommen, "Models of Ministry," p. 85.
19. The Supreme Court in *Roe v. Wade* and *Doe v. Bolton* (1973) put the decision for abortion within the purview of the woman's right of privacy and hence, as a personal matter between the woman and her physician.
20. Coburn, *Minister: Man-in-the-Middle,* pp. 28, 150; Harmon, *Ministerial Ethics and Etiquette,* p. 137; and Switzer, *Pastor, Preacher, Person,* p. 18.
21. Southard, *Pastoral Authority,* p. 7.
22. Ibid., p. 8.
23. E.g., Hulme relies on commitment or character to "provide the inner strength to control his actions," in the face of temptation. *Your Pastor's Problems,* p. 88.
24. Pellegrino, *Humanism and the Physician,* chap. 6.
25. Bok, *Secrets,* p. 86.
26. Cf. Peter Berger and Thomas Luckmann, *The Social Construction of Reality* (Garden City, N.J.: Doubleday, 1966).
27. Hughes, "Professions," p. 2.
28. Ibid.
29. Freidson, *Profession of Medicine,* p. xvii.
30. Menninger, *Whatever Became of Sin?,* p. 53.
31. Cogan, "Toward a Definition of Profession," pp. 33-50.
32. Menninger, *Whatever Became of Sin?,* p. 54.
33. H. Tristram Engelhardt, Jr., "The Disease of Masturbation: Values and the Concept of Disease," in Tom Beauchamp and LeRoy Walters, eds., *Contemporary Issues in Bioethics,* 2d ed. (Belmont, Calif.: Wadsworth Publishing Co., 1982), pp. 59ff.; see also Thomas Szasz, *Sex by Prescription* (New York: Penguin Books, 1980).
34. Cf. C. O. Carter, "Practical Aspects of Early Diagnosis," in Maureen Harris, ed., *Early Diagnosis of Human Genetic Defects: Scientific and Ethical Considerations* (U.S. Government Printing Office, 1972), pp. 18-19.
35. Cf. Hughes, "Professions," p. 3: "Only the professional can say when his colleague makes a mistake." See also Freidson, *Profession of Medicine.*
36. Cf. H. Tristram Engelhardt, Jr., "Illnesses, Diseases, and Sicknesses," in Victor Kestenbaum, ed., *The Humanity of the Ill: Phenomenological Perspectives* (Knoxville: University of Tennessee Press, 1982), pp. 142-56.
37. Menninger, *Whatever Became of Sin?;* see also Hauerwas, *Vision and Virtue,* p. 46.
38. Janice Riggle Huey, "Preaching Through Metaphor," in Weidman, *Women Ministers,* p. 51.
39. Russell, *Future of Partnership,* p. 152.
40. Cornwall, *Your Daughters Shall Prophesy,* p. 108.
41. Coburn, *Minister: Man-in-the-Middle,* p. 194.
42. Ibid., p. 140.
43. Bayles, *Professional Ethics,* p. 69.

44. Southard, *Pastoral Authority*, p. 8; cf. Strain, *Measure of a Minister*, p. 112.
45. Hulme, *Your Pastor's Problems*, p. 98.
46. David S. Viscott, *The Making of a Psychiatrist* (Greenwich, Conn.: Fawcett Publications, 1972), p. 193.
47. Carlton, *"In Our Professional Opinion . . ."*
48. C. Wright Mills, *Power, Politics and People* (New York: Oxford University Press, 1963), chap. 7; cf. Roland L. Warren, "The Sociology of Knowledge and the Problems of the Inner Cities," *Social Science Quarterly* (1971).
49. Cf. Jean Baker Miller, *Toward a New Psychology of Women* (Boston: Beacon Press, 1976).

8. Justice and Liberation

1. Cf. Barber, "Regulation and the Professions," p. 34; see also Carr-Saunders and Wilson, *The Professions*, p. 284.
2. Barber, "Regulation and the Professions"; see also B. B. Page, "Who Owns the Professions?" *The Hastings Center Report* 5, no. 5 (October 1975): 7.
3. H. R. Moody, "Demythologizing the Professionals," *Christianity and Crisis* 31, no. 5 (5 April 1971): 54.
4. Ibid., p. 55.
5. Michael D. Bayles, "Against Professional Autonomy," *National Forum* 58, no. 3 (1978): 23-26.
6. Newton, "A Professional Ethic," p. 266.
7. Ibid., p. 267.
8. Russell, *Future of Partnership*, p. 134.
9. Newton, "A Professional Ethic," p. 269; a similar proposal is made by Page, "Who Owns the Professions?" p. 8.
10. Beverly W. Harrison and W. Robert Martin, Jr., "Is Theological Education Good for Any Woman's Health?" *Newsletter of The Center for Women and Religion* 4, no. 2 (Winter 1978): 6-10; for similar views on the exclusion of women in health professions, see Jo Ann Ashley, *Hospitals, Paternalism and the Role of the Nurse* (New York: Teachers College Press, 1977), and Mary Roth Walsh, *"Doctors Wanted: No Women Need Apply": Sexual Barriers in the Medical Profession 1835–1975* (New Haven: Yale University Press, 1977).
11. Southard, *Pastoral Authority*, p. 13.
12. Barbara J. Harris, *Beyond Her Sphere: Women and the Professions in American History* (Westport, Conn.: Greenwood Press, 1978), p. 117.
13. Judith L. Weidman, "Introduction," in Weidman, ed., *Women Ministers*, p. 3.
14. Harrison and Martin, "Is Theological Education Good for Any Woman's Health?" p. 10.
15. Cornwall, *Your Daughters Shall Prophesy*.
16. Russell, *Future of Partnership*, p. 126.
17. Ibid., p. 127.
18. Bok, *Lying*, p. 18.

19. Ibid., pp. 20-22.
20. Surprisingly little has been written on biblical and Christian perspectives on justice. For a review of the Catholic tradition on social justice, see David J. O'Brien and Thomas A. Shannon, eds., *Renewing the Earth: Catholic Documents on Peace, Justice and Liberation* (New York: Doubleday, 1977). For a contemporary Catholic perspective, see Daniel C. McGuire, *A New American Justice: Ending the White Male Monopolies* (New York: Doubleday, 1980). A Protestant perspective is offered by John Howard Yoder in *The Politics of Jesus* (Grand Rapids: Wm. B. Eerdmans Publishing Co., 1972). And biblical excerpts on issues related to justice can be found in Ronald J. Sider, ed., *Cry Justice: The Bible on Hunger and Poverty* (New York: Paulist Press, 1980).
21. Russell, *Future of Partnership*, p. 153.
22. Cf. James H. Cone, *A Black Theology of Liberation* (New York: J. B. Lippincott, 1970), and Allan Aubrey Boesak, *Farewell to Innocence: A Socio-Ethical Study on Black Theology and Power* (Maryknoll, N.Y.: Orbis Books, 1977). Numerous other liberation theologians have linked issues of power, justice, and liberation. See, for example, Gerald H. Anderson and Thomas F. Stransky, C.S.P., eds., *Mission Trends 3: Third World Theologies* (New York: Paulist Press, 1976), and *Mission Trends 4: Liberation Theologies.*
23. Cornwall, *Your Daughters Shall Prophesy,* p. 96.
24. Ibid., p. 110.
25. Gill, "Ministry of Presence," p. 100.
26. Ibid., p. 104.
27. Russell, *Future of Partnership,* p. 134.
28. Pellegrino, *Humanism and the Physician,* p. 117; my emphasis.
29. Ibid., p. 123.
30. Russell, *Future of Partnership,* p. 137; see also Gross, "Embodied Church," p. 150.
31. Reeck, *Ethics for the Professions,* p. 38; see also Otano-Rivera, "Task of Enabling," p. 165.
32. The women's movement has given considerable attention to the subtle ways in which imbalances of power are communicated and maintained. See, for example, Jo Freeman, ed., *Women: A Feminist Perspective,* 2d ed. (Palo Alto: Mayfield Publishing Co., 1979).
33. Cf. Harmon, *Ministerial Ethics and Etiquette,* p. 98.
34. Coburn, *Minister: Man-in-the-Middle,* p. 147.
35. Pellegrino, *Humanism and the Physician,* p. 113.
36. The situation described here is drawn from an actual case presented by the Reverend David Huntington. For an additional analysis of the impact of structures on the delivery of care, see Rose Laub Coser, "Alienation and the Social Structure: Case Analysis of a Hospital," in David Tuckett and Joseph M. Kaufert, eds., *Basic Readings in Medical Sociology* (London: Tavistock Publications, 1978), pp. 213-22.
37. For a happy exception that comes close to discussing these issues, see Jonsen and Hellegers, "Conceptual Foundations for an Ethics of Medical Care," pp. 3-20.
38. Emmet, *Rules, Roles and Relations,* chap. 9.

9. Power and Paradox

1. Gaye Tuchman, "Women's Depiction by the Mass Media," *Signs* 4, no. 3 (Spring 1979): 535.
2. The Cornwall Collective defines sexism as "a set of attitudes, behaviors and societal structures that differentiate between men and women on the basis of their sex in access to resources, participation in making and enforcing decisions, setting criteria for inclusion/exclusion . . . , [and] the power to name reality." See *Your Daughters Shall Prophesy*, p. xiii.
3. See Bosk, *Forgive and Remember;* see also Carlton, *"In Our Professional Opinion . . ."*
4. Freidson, *Profession of Medicine*, p. 90.
5. Ibid., p. 89.
6. Coser, "Alienation and the Social Structure: Case Analysis of a Hospital," pp. 213-22.
7. Prestwood, *New Breed of Clergy*, p. 31.
8. David S. Schuller, "Basic Issues in Defining Ministry," in Schuller, Strommen, and Brekke, *Ministry in America*, p. 8.
9. James W. Kennedy, *Ministers' Shop-Talk*, p. 56.
10. Gustafson, "Clergy in the United States," pp. 70-90; see also John C. Harris, *Stress, Power and Ministry* (Washington, D.C.: The Alban Institute, 1977).
11. Russell, *Future of Partnership*, p. 128.
12. In this respect, although ministers are considered part of the "learned" professions, they are not unlike the "consulting" professions. Cf. Freidson, *Profession of Medicine*, p. 74.
13. Gustafson, "Clergy in the United States," pp. 81-82; cf. Southard, *Pastoral Authority*, pp. 33-39.
14. Jud, et al., *Ex-Pastors*, p. 65.
15. This is also true in medicine, nursing, and other professions where an increasing amount of professional time is spent in paperwork and administrative detail.
16. Holmes, *Future Shape of Ministry*, p. 141.
17. Donald P. Smith, *Clergy in the Cross Fire*, p. 48.
18. Prestwood, *New Breed of Clergy*, p. 59.
19. Strommen, "Models of Ministry," pp. 73-78.
20. Prestwood, *New Breed of Clergy*, p. 28.
21. Gerald Kennedy, *The Seven Worlds of the Minister* (New York: Harper & Row, 1968), p. 75.
22. The importance of professional organizations was lifted up as early as 1933 in the classic study by Carr-Saunders and Wilson, *The Professions*, p. 298: "A profession can only be said to exist when there are bonds between the practitioners and these bonds can take but one shape—that of formal association." The lack of professional association for ministers is noted by Glasse in *Profession: Minister;* Glasse argues that parish clergy need a professional association precisely in order to give them professional power.
23. This may be why no codes of ethics for ministers appear among the more than two hundred such codes provided by Clapp in *Professional Ethics and Insignia*.

24. Cf. Russell, *Future of Partnership*, p. 128.
25. Cf. Pollock, "Growing Toward Effective Ministry," p. 18; and Switzer, *Pastor, Preacher, Person*, p. 27.
26. Jud, et al., *Ex-Pastors*, p. 85.
27. Ibid., p. 53.
28. Ibid., p. 85.
29. Park, "Women and Liturgy," p. 82.
30. Hulme, *Your Pastor's Problems*, p. 19.
31. Jud, et al., "Few professionals are as visible in all their actions as are clergymen." *Ex-Pastors*, p. 86.
32. Indeed, Coburn suggests that "it is still not unheard of for parishioners to walk unannounced into the parsonage because the house 'belongs to us.'" See *Minister: Man-in-the-Middle*, p. 186.
33. Marilyn Brown Oden, *The Minister's Wife: Person or Position?* (Nashville: Abingdon Press, 1966), p. 34.
34. Bayles, *Professional Ethics*, p. 118.
35. Russell, *Future of Partnership*, p. 129.
36. Glasse, *Profession: Minister*, p. 130.
37. Cf. Brandon, *Pastor and His Ministry*.
38. Harris, *Stress, Power and Ministry*, chap. 5.
39. See Gannon, "Priest/Minister: Profession or Non-Profession?" pp. 66-79; Peter Jarvis, "The Ministry: Occupation, Profession or Status?" pp. 264-67.
40. Russell, *Future of Partnership*, pp. 76, 71; Cornwall, *Your Daughters Shall Prophesy*, p. 29.
41. For an important perspective on the particular problems this creates for women, see Margaret Adams, "The Compassion Trap," in Vivian Gornick and Barbara K. Moran, eds., *Woman in Sexist Society: Studies in Power and Powerlessness* (New York: Basic Books, 1971), pp. 555-75.
42. Schuller, "Basic Issues in Defining Ministry," p. 4.
43. This is an actual case shared by a former student in my course on professional ethics.
44. Cf. Guggenbühl-Craig, *Power in the Helping Professions*.

Conclusion: Croquet and Confidentiality

1. The current literature on women's oppression is massive. See, for example, Freeman, *Women: A Feminist Perspective*, 2d ed.; also Gornick and Moran, *Woman in Sexist Society*.
2. Cf. Stanley Hauerwas, *A Community of Character: Toward a Constructive Christian Social Ethic* (Notre Dame, Ind.: University of Notre Dame Press, 1981), p. 201.
3. Cf. Beverly Wildung Harrison, *Our Right to Choose: Toward a New Ethic of Abortion* (Boston: Beacon Press, 1983).
4. See, for example, Carol Gilligan, *In a Different Voice: Psychological Theory and Women's Development* (Cambridge, Mass.: Harvard University Press, 1982); the pattern of victimization is also described by Gross in "Embodied Church," p. 141.
5. Cornwall, *Your Daughters Shall Prophesy*, p. 96. The confrontive language of liberation is generally proposed between oppressor and

oppressed. Here, I am proposing that it can be used in a therapeutic context to facilitate recognition of oppression on the part of the oppressed.

6. Cf. Hauerwas, *Truthfulness and Tragedy,* p. 35.

7. Hauerwas argues that the Christian story has always been opposed to abortion. See *Community of Character,* chaps. 11, 12. Harrison argues, however, that a true reading of the Christian story does not necessarily yield the anti-abortion bias that Hauerwas assumes. See Harrison, *Our Right to Choose,* chap. 6.

8. Bok, *Secrets,* p. 125.

9. Ibid., p. 106.

10. Bayles argues that there are six role-specific duties of the professional and that those other than clients are not owed all six of these duties but only the three duties of truthfulness, non-harming, and fairness. See Bayles, *Professional Ethics,* p. 94. Here, however, ministers are in a slightly different position from other professionals since they have both the role-specific obligations that go with undertaking a specific counseling setting and also the role-specific obligations that derive from their role as a generalist in ministry.

11. Dyck, *On Human Care,* chap. 5.

12. Cf. Joseph L. Allen, *Love and Conflict: A Covenantal Model of Christian Ethics* (Nashville: Abingdon Press, 1984), chap. 5.

13. Coburn, *Minister: Man-in-the-Middle,* p. 21.

14. Cf. Bok, *Secrets,* p. 117.

15. William F. May, "Notes on the Ethics of Doctors and Lawyers," p. 12.

16. Cornwall, *Your Daughters Shall Prophesy,* p. 97.

17. California Supreme Court, *Tarasoff v. Regents of the University of California* (131 California Reporter 14, 1976); see also Bok, *Secrets,* chap. 9.

18. Legal access to abortion was secured by the decisions of the United States Supreme Court in *Roe v. Wade* and *Doe v. Bolton* in 1973.

19. Cf. Hauerwas, *Vision and Virtue,* at p. 117: "A Christian ethic is ultimately an ethic of truth or it is neither Christian nor an ethic substantive enough to deal with the human condition."

INDEX

abortion, 9, 28, 29, 80, 84, 115, 119, 131, 155, 160, 164; legality of, 162; and liberation, 154; and right to life, 162

acts: and character, 83-85, 93; continuity of , 78-83; meaning of, 96-101, 106, 150, 163; private, 97-98; public, 98; reasons for, 97, 99, 100, 163

Alice in Wonderland, 11

American Dental Association, 67

aretaic judgments. *See* virtues

Association of Theological Schools (ATS), 49, 64, 140, 143, 147

authority, 53, 65, 113, 121, 146, 160; of ministers, 141-46; source of, 89; and structures, 137-46. *See also* power

autonomy, 51, 132, 133, 150, 155; of professionals, 65, 87, 88, 119, 125, 127, 135, 144-45, 148; *See also* liberation

Barber, Bernard, 87

Bayles, Michael, 19, 37, 42, 50, 74, 79, 120, 125, 126, 146

being. *See* character; identification with role; virtues

beneficence, 25, 70, 75, 98, 103, 129, 153

betrayal, 90, 102, 159

Body of Christ, 19, 157

Bok, Sissela, 17, 113, 116, 128, 155

Bosk, Charles, 53

Brandon, Owen, 64

Calian, C. S., 69-70

calling, 64-69

Carlton, Wendy, 53

Carr-Saunders, A. M. and Wilson, P. A., 68-69, 70, 71, 75

case study: ministers' reflections on, 41, 42, 75, 80, 82, 85, 157

character: and acts, 78-84, 100, 163; and definition of situation, 78; as role expectation of ministers, 152; traits of, 92. *See also* virtues

church: characteristics of, 141, 143, 144

clothes, 48, 135

clown: as model for ministry, 51

codes of ethics, 66, 68, 113; and character, 68, 73, 75, 83, 86, 88, 124; critique of, 66-67, 135; in ministry, 10, 15, 143; and obligations, 32, 42, 65-71, 75

Cogan, Morris, 118

commitment, 49, 65, 69, 73, 147

community: requisites for, 22

compassion, 53

competence, 51, 53, 56, 68-70, 73, 74, 83

confession, 16-17, 113

confidentiality, 38, 79, 80, 81, 82, 133, 149, 158, 159, 164; breaking, 72, 82, 85, 155, 157-62; defined, 156; reasons for, 16-17, 39, 73, 75-76, 91, 154-56; required of professionals, 15, 17, 23, 32, 42, 68, 69, 70, 89, 124

consequences, 17, 20, 21, 25. *See also* situation ethics
Cornwall Collective, 99, 127, 129, 130, 161
Coser, Rose Laub, 139
covenant, 50, 84, 90, 157, 161. *See also* models

deception: self-, 85, 98, 154
dedication. *See* commitment
defensiveness, 98
definition of reality, 116-20, 121, 127, 131, 138, 148, 153, 160. *See also* power: of professionals
definition of situation, 23, 128. *See also* acts: meaning of
deontology, 22
Didion, Joan, 49, 100
discernment, 28-29, 96, 104, 149, 150, 152. *See also* prudence
Douglas, Ann, 45
duties. *See* deontology; prima facie duties; role expectations
duty to divulge, 161-62
Dyck, Arthur, 95

education. *See* training
Emmet, Dorothy, 33, 71, 73, 75, 136
empowerment. *See* liberation
enablement. *See* liberation
ethical dilemma: defined, 77
etiquette, 66-67, 70, 71
experience, 105

fairness. *See* justice
faithfulness: of God, 90; as virtue, *see* trustworthiness
family: role expectations of minister's, 145
fidelity. *See* trustworthiness
Fletcher, Joseph, 20, 22, 23, 24
forgiveness. *See* sin
Fourth Lateran Council, 16
framework: for decision making, 10-12, 152
Frankena, William, 78
Freidson, Eliot, 117, 139
Fried, Charles, 110

friendship: as model for professionals, 110-14; role expectations in, 81
function: as part of image, 48

Gill, Brita, 89, 130
God, 47, 51, 84, 87, 89, 90, 105, 113, 115, 120, 127, 141
"good Joe," 56
good Samaritan, 103
Goodfield, June, 66
gratitude, 25, 37, 94
Guggenbühl-Craig, Adolf, 98
Gustafson, James, 22, 29, 64

Hackler, Chris, 40
harm. *See* non-maleficence
Harmon, Nolan, 63
Harris, Barbara, 127
Harrison, Beverly, 127
Hauerwas, Stanley, 98, 101, 120, 165
heroes, 79
Hippocratic Oath, 46
Holmes, Sherlock, 55-56
Holmes, Urban, 65
honesty, 70, 79, 124. *See also* truth telling
honor: as commandment, 157; as virtue, 76, 79, 97
Hughes, Everett, 116
Hulme, William, 48, 64, 105, 110
humility, 64, 65, 74

identification with role, 35, 71, 74, 145-46
images: and character, 64, 70, 79; and power, 121, 139, 148; and role expectations, 47-49, 54, 55, 58, 68, 72, 97, 152; vs. reality in ministry, 140-46. *See also* suffering servant
imitation of Christ, 102
individualism, 122
inefficiency, 51
informed consent. *See* respect for persons
institutions and professional practice, 112

parenthood: ministers' perceptions of, 158; as model for professionals, 109-14; rights of parents, 156-59; role expectations in, 33, 38, 45, 83-85

Park, Patricia, 48, 144

parsonage: effect on role, 145

Parsons, Talcott, 87

partnership: as model for ministry, 51, 146

pastor. *See* ministerial role

paternalism, 87, 110, 131, 150

Pellegrino, Edmund, 73, 116, 130-31, 136

perception: checks and balances on, 158-59, 161; factors affecting, 53, 95, 100, 138, 158; parables as guide to, 103

Pieper, Josef, 104

Pollock, Helene, 55

power: and authority, 113, 114; checks on, 87, 124-25, 127; desire for, 98, 99, 150; normative implications, 113, 128, 136, 160, 161; paradoxical, 146-48; of professionals, 87, 110, 113-18, 119, 121, 126, 146-47, 153, 156; and structures, 133, 137-46, 150, 160

power gap, 119, 121, 130, 131-33, 149, 153

praxis, 10

prayer, 105-6, 158. *See also* prudence

Prestwood, Charles, 140, 142, 143

priest-penitent privilege, 16, 156

prima facie duties, 24-28, 77, 94, 152, 153, 163; and duty proper, 24; justification for breaking, 38-39; and professional role, 31-33, 37-40; reflected in codes, 70, 75

primum non nocere, 33, 46, 57

principles. *See* rules

professional organizations, 143-44, 146

professionalism, 71, 125

professions, 64, 73, 87, 99, 117, 127; characteristics of, 65;

critique of, 125. *See also* ministry

promise keeping, 21-22, 25, 26, 28, 40-41, 50, 75, 80, 88. *See also* trustworthiness

prophet. *See* ministerial role

prudence, 104-6, 153, 158. *See also* virtues

racism, 99, 102, 105

Ramsey, Paul, 80

reconciliation, 158-59

redemption. *See* sin

Reeck, Darrell, 104, 131

repentance. *See* sin

respect for persons, 25, 28, 67, 74, 157

Rich, Adrienne, 17, 90

right to life, 20

role expectations: ambiguity in, 35, 54-55, 56, 57, 146; and character, 152; conflict in, 54-58, 68, 140; nature and origins of, 35-40, 44, 45, 46, 49, 54, 58, 84, 112, 152; of professionals, 42, 55, 57, 72, 129, 143, 145. *See also* friendship; ministerial role; parenthood

role models, 49, 52

roles, 33-40, 45-47, 58, 59, 73, 96; role-holder, 44, 47; role-set, 144

Ross, W. D., 24, 25, 26, 27, 30

rules: and character, 70, 82, 103; justifying exceptions to, 16-18, 23, 26, 32, 38, 99; nature, origins, and use of, 15-24, 40, 52, 58, 77, 152; problems with, 78, 81, 82; for professionals, 30, 32, 106, 156

Russell, Letty, 51, 110, 126, 128, 129, 130, 146

Ruth (biblical story), 86

salvation. *See* ministerial role

seal of the confessional, 16, 156

secrecy. *See* confidentiality

service, 64, 65, 68-70, 124, 147

sexism, 99, 102, 105, 138

"sick role," 33